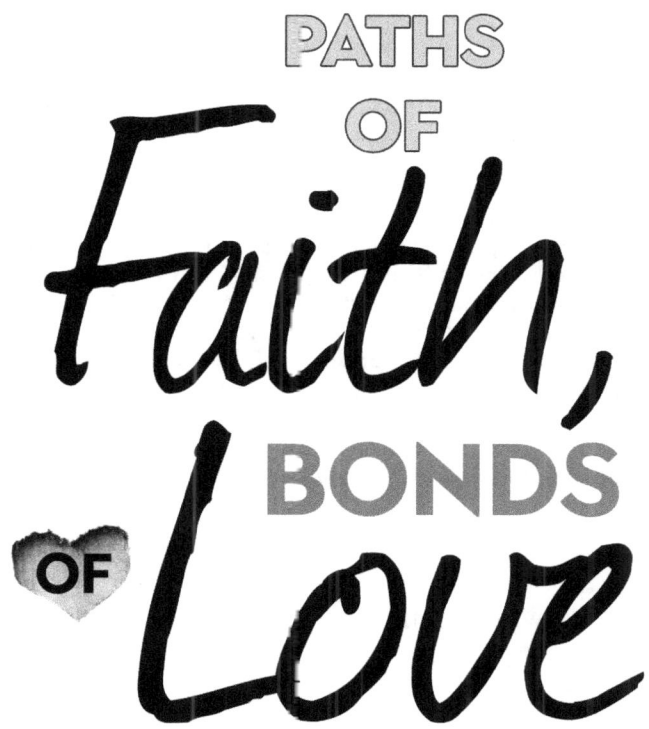

JIM BELL

PATH OF FAITH, BONDS OF LOVE
Copyright © 2024 by Jim Bell

All rights reserved. Neither this publication nor any part of this publication may be reproduced or transmitted in any form or by any means, electronic or mechanical, including photocopying, recording or any information storage and retrieval system, without permission in writing from the author.

The content of this publication is based on actual events. Names may have been changed to protect individual privacy.

Unless otherwise indicated, scripture quotations are taken from THE HOLY BIBLE, NEW INTERNATIONAL VERSION®, NIV® Copyright © 1973, 1978, 1984, 2011 by Biblica, Inc.® Used by permission. All rights reserved worldwide. • Scripture quotations marked (ESV) are taken from the ESV® Bible (The Holy Bible, English Standard Version®). ESV® Text Edition: 2016. Copyright © 2001 by Crossway, a publishing ministry of Good News Publishers. The ESV® text has been reproduced in cooperation with and by permission of Good News Publishers. Unauthorized reproduction of this publication is prohibited. All rights reserved. • Scripture quotations marked (NLT) are taken from Holy Bible, New Living Translation, copyright © 1996, 2004, 2015 by Tyndale House Foundation. Used by permission of Tyndale House Publishers, Inc., Carol Stream, Illinois 60188. All rights reserved.

ISBN: 978-1-4866-2603-8

Word Alive Press
119 De Baets Street Winnipeg, MB R2J 3R9
www.wordalivepress.ca

Cataloguing in Publication information can be obtained from Library and Archives Canada.

CONTENTS

FOREWORD		v
Introduction: **WHY AM I DOING THIS?**		vii
One:	**RECOLLECTIONS FROM CHILDHOOD**	1
Two:	**THE FOUNDATIONAL YEARS**	13
Three:	**FALLING IN LOVE, STAYING IN LOVE**	25
Four:	**THOSE EARLY DAYS OF OUR MARRIAGE**	37
Five:	**THE COTTAGE—OUR LITTLE PIECE OF HEAVEN**	45
Six:	**A PASSION FOR THE GAME**	49
Seven:	**A TOUCH FOOTBALL ODYSSEY**	59
Eight:	**"A BAND OF BROTHERS"**	67
Nine:	**MY WORK EXPERIENCES**	79
Ten:	**TRAGEDY, CHALLENGES, AND CHANGES**	97
Eleven:	**A NEW STADIUM—WHAT A PROJECT!**	105
Twelve:	**A TRUE FRIEND AND COLLEAGUE**	111

Thirteen:	**NEVER SAY NEVER—A RUN AT POLITICS**	117
Fourteen:	**A NEW CHALLENGE—SILOAM MISSION**	125
Fifteen:	**PASSAGES**	139
Sixteen:	**GENERATIONAL TREASURES**	145
Seventeen:	**HELEN—MY BEST FRIEND AND SOULMATE**	161
The Last Chapter—**OR IS IT?**		163
Afterword:	**TO MY FAMILY AND FRIENDS**	165

A NOTE TO GOD	169
APPENDIX I	171
APPENDIX II	177
APPENDIX III	181
APPENDIX IV	183
APPENDIX V	185

FOREWORD

IT'S A PROFOUND honour to pen the foreword for Jim's deeply personal and heartfelt memoir. As I journeyed through these pages, I felt as though I'd been granted a rare and privileged invitation into the sacred space of a family's home on Christmas morning, witnessing the intimate moments of joy, love, and reflection that accompany the unwrapping of cherished gifts.

This memoir, intricately woven with the tapestry of relationships, beautifully captures the essence of a life rich in love and connection. Jim's love for his wife, children, and grandchildren shines brightly, like the guiding star of his journey. Each chapter reveals the depth of these bonds, exploring the friendships and partnerships that have touched Jim's life. Every relationship is a vibrant thread that weaves together the fabric of his story, creating a vivid mosaic of human experience.

Jim's narrative bravely embraces the full spectrum of his experiences. Alongside his many career successes, he shares candidly his disappointments and the challenges he faced. It's this raw honesty that makes his story so compelling and relatable, revealing the resilience and perseverance that have shaped his remarkable journey.

When Jim joined Silcam Mission, I had the unique privilege of working alongside him during this pivotal transition. As the retiring CEO, I stayed on for a few weeks to offer a helping hand to Jim and introduce him to Siloam. During this time, I witnessed firsthand his kindness, wisdom, and eagerness to learn. Jim's humility and openness were evident as we toured the Siloam operations, met the dedicated team, and interacted with the individuals we served. These initial weeks were marked by Jim's genuine desire to understand and connect with everyone, laying the foundation for the deep relationships he would form.

I hold the utmost respect for Jim, not only for his professional acumen but also for his personal virtues. His wisdom is profound, yet he carries it with a humility that is both rare and admirable. Jim's strong faith is the cornerstone of his character, guiding his actions and decisions with unwavering integrity. His ability to inspire and lead with compassion is a testament to the strength of his convictions and the depth of his love for those around him.

Woven throughout this narrative is Jim's profound devotion to Jesus. His faith is not merely a backdrop but a guiding force, infusing his experiences with purpose and meaning. It's through this lens of faith that he navigates the joys and sorrows, the triumphs and trials, offering readers a testament to the power of spiritual devotion in shaping a life of integrity and love.

In sharing these memoirs, Jim opens his heart and soul to us, allowing us to witness the moments that have defined him. His stories aren't just recollections of the past but lessons for the present, offering wisdom and insight into the complexities of human relationships and the enduring power of faith.

As you immerse yourself in these pages, may you be inspired by the depth of Jim's love, the strength of his convictions, and the beauty of the relationships that have enriched his life. This memoir is a gift, a reminder of the importance of cherishing those we hold dear and finding strength in our faith.

—Garry Corbett, PhD, CDMP, CVRP(D), CCVE(D), VRAC(F)

Introduction

WHY AM I DOING THIS?

A STIRRING WITHIN me has prompted the start of this endeavour—to write. This thought has lingered for some time. This venture is unlike anything I've undertaken before; I've never felt the urge for it. Journaling has never been my forte.

As I embark on this writing journey, I lack a concrete plan. Perhaps it's my yearning to ponder life, to peer ahead. The destination isn't clear, but that's the beauty of it. Maybe age is the catalyst; now in my mid-sixties, it feels like the right time. (Note: I started this project in my late fifties, and as I review this now, I'm sixty-five. This has been a lengthy undertaking, well worth the time spent.) Time to reflect. Time to anticipate. Where has time vanished? What have I learned? What holds significance along life's convoluted path? Am I grateful? Do I rest content within myself? Numerous questions arise. I can't list them all, but I hope to address a few. Will writing and reflecting provide answers? Uncertainty looms, but it's an endeavour worth pursuing.

To whoever reads this—whether family, close friend, or stranger—know that I recognize the blessings in my life. It hasn't been a life devoid of challenges. Life's trials are universal, and I've faced my share. I'm sure you have as well. I like to walk, and I do it a lot. Have you ever embarked on a leisurely stroll, alone or with loved ones, and encountered varied paths? Some are straightforward, others wide; both offer foresight. But occasionally, a path bends unexpectedly, or a storm arises. Life mirrors this unpredictability. Life is an imperfect journey strewn with paths both smooth and rugged. You might describe it differently, but I believe you understand.

I've relished joyful moments and cherished the lighter aspects of life's journey. Adversity, however, is not as welcome. Yet I acknowledge the value in confronting life's challenges, even if learning through adversity isn't always enjoyable. Who embraces hardship? These thoughts recall a Bible passage about hope, character, and perseverance: Romans 5:3–5. It speaks of tribulations fostering perseverance and character, leading to hope. These words resonate with me, and their truth is inspiring. Pause, read it again. Consider its relevance to your journey. Do these verses echo in your life?

But I digress; let's continue. The grammar and anecdotes that follow are equally imperfect. Whether you read a snippet or the whole, I hope you find enjoyment. Perhaps my stories resonate, and if so, feel free to engage. Challenge me, question me—whether laughter or tears arise, or curiosity takes hold. Imagine us conversing over coffee, sharing our unique journeys. I would like that very much. By the way, I like my coffee strong, with just a hint of cream. Throw in a chocolate chip cookie or two and you really have my attention. My aspiration is to learn through this process, inspiring others to reflect too. Life offers one chance on this Earth—a profound thought. Another query: What is my purpose here anyway?

I hope to address some questions, even the unspoken ones. That's my goal: candid reflection. My life has been imperfect, and you'll witness it through these pages. Triumphs and trials shape my narrative. Regrets linger, decisions shine. Such is life. One more consideration: honesty. As I recount memories and experiences, honesty guides me. My path is marked by both wisdom and blunders. And when I say wisdom, I have relied heavily on the wisdom of others. For a deeper understanding, consult my wife, Helen, and my children. They'll paint a full picture of my love and flaws.

An entire book could be written on my imperfections! Helen, Trevor, Cory, and Acksanna, I hope you're gentle if approached about this, but please be honest. I will not be offended. I extend the same offer to those who know me best, and you know who you are!

One constant accompanies me: God. His love and presence endure daily. A childhood song, "Jesus Loves Me," echoes in my heart, taught by my Grandma Bell. A humble melody from Harstone United Church's Sunday school. Funny, the memories we carry.

God's unwavering love emboldens me. The lyrics of a song "If We're Honest" encapsulate this sentiment: If we're honest, we know that we're broken; however, love can heal and mercy awaits us. We need to be honest and vulnerable too.

So I write with an intention: honesty and vulnerability. I don't claim perfection—far from it. One thing I know is that God's companionship is unwavering. His love encompasses all, including me. "Jesus loves me"—my grandma's lesson, my foundational truth. It rings in my ears as I begin to write and reflect. May my words prove worthwhile for me and those who read.

One

RECOLLECTIONS FROM CHILDHOOD

I WAS BORN on July 28, 1959, in Winnipeg, Manitoba. Just for kicks, I checked the history books for that day and it was hot, got to almost thirty-six degrees Celsius. I know, totally useless information!

At the age of around f ve, my memories become vivid, and they take me back to a place that holds a special significance—1077 Dominion Street in Winnipeg's west end. A visual snapshot remains of my Grandma Bell's presence next door at 1079 Dominion Street. However, my initial days on this planet were spent at The Thunderbird Apartments on Portage Avenue in St. James, and I've seen glimpses of our inaugural home on Sherburn Street, a mere two streets east of Dominion.

Flickers of kindergarten at Sargent Park School paint a vibrant picture. Mrs. Fediuk, my first teacher, left an indelible mark, and her recent obituary highlighted her spiritual nature. It's intriguing to ponder whether she planted seeds of spirituality with n me. Sargent Park School, conveniently nestled directly across the street from our home, cultivated some of my most cherished memories during those tender years.

Growing up on Dominion Street unfolded like an adventure. Friendships flourished, driven by a shared fervor for sports. The names Jeff, Al, Bernie, and others emerge as snapshots of those who joined my journey. Interestingly enough, Al and I bumped into each other while golfing in the summer of 2022, a reunion after over four decades. The memories of our shared paper route on Dominion Street resurfaced, and I'm reminded of Al's prowess as the standout athlete among us.

My home on the right, growing up on Dominion Street. That's my grandma's house next door on the left.

Amid these friends on Dominion Street, one name echoes more profoundly—Tim, who would later become my closest friend. Tim and I wouldn't meet until a few years later, and I plan on writing more about our friendship. Our daily rendezvous in the schoolyard for games—football, ball hockey, soccer—formed the canvas of our youthful aspirations. Our imaginative play, donning the roles of Blue Bombers players such as Don Jonas, Ken Neilsen, and Ed Ulmer, resonates even now. The crowd's imaginary cheers echo as the ball was thrown, caught, or kicked. Those innocent days of dream-filled play still echo in my memory.

Sargent Park School's significance transcends its geographical proximity to our house. Exceptional teachers left their imprint, guiding me through my formative years. Mrs. Fediuk, Mrs. Gill, Mrs. Kettle, Mrs. Ferdette, Miss Chimchack (with a fondness for cats), Mr. Ward (our soccer coach), Mrs. Hamlin, Mr. Zagrodnik, and Mr. Buckingham—they all played their part in my elementary education.

My first school, Sargent Park where I attended kindergarten through grade 9. Right across the street from our house.

This used to be my playground, the schoolyard at Sargent Park School. That's me, standing, there in the summer of 2022. Nobody has more footprints here than me!.

Among these memories, one from grade 3, with Mrs. Ferdette, stands out. Mathematics was my forte, and a special visit from Mr. Froese, a math teacher from Daniel McIntyre High School, validated my skills. Mr. Froese conducted a speed test that day, and I did exceptionally well. Earning praise for outperforming 70 per cent of grade 5 students bolstered my confidence and likely influenced my subsequent career path in accounting and finance.

Sports emerged as a cornerstone of my life from a tender age. The schoolyard transformed into my training ground, fostering my engagement in soccer, volleyball, basketball, and hockey teams throughout my journey until grade 9. These experiences etched enduring lessons on teamwork, trust, and leadership.

Transitioning to junior high at Sargent Park School brought new chapters of growth. The strict yet respected Mr. Kozoris, Miss Osiowy, and Mrs. Ryan enriched my education and character. The realm of school sports continued to captivate me, nurturing my passion for competition and collaboration. In the annals of my schooling, grade 9 retains a prominent spot. Triumph arrived when I emerged victorious in the school tennis tournament, an achievement that defined my status as the best player. This success planted the seed of a competitive spirit, an enduring trait that still thrives within me. To this day I play sports to compete, and I play to win, for which I make no apologies. Memories of these formative years, painted with friendships, sportsmanship, and learning, remain an integral part of my journey.

Growing Up

Growing up in the west end of Winnipeg was an enjoyable and memorable experience. Dominion Street, while not my first home, remains the most vivid and memorable in my mind.

As an only child, I navigated the ups and downs of growing up without siblings. While I was quite content and couldn't imagine anything different, I occasionally pondered what having a brother or sister would be like. Did I miss something growing up, not having a sibling? I admit to thinking about this from time to time. That changed significantly in later years, a story I'll delve into when I turn twenty-two.

My father was a skilled stucco worker. Dad came from a large family; he had eight siblings. He had two brothers, one older and one younger, along with six sisters. One of his sisters was his twin. His two brothers were in business together and became extremely wealthy.

Our family gatherings were lively and often comedic affairs, full of spirited aunts, uncles, and cousins. Thanksgiving at Aunt Jean's or Aunt Marjorie's was particularly enjoyable. I recall a memorable Thanksgiving at Aunt Marjorie's where we engaged in touch football before feasting on my aunt's incredible cooking. Quality time with family was invaluable.

My mother, originally from Northern Ireland, came to Canada in the mid-1950s. Her Irish accent has remained as thick as ever, adding a charming touch to our household. She worked at Old Dutch Foods throughout my youth and beyond, demonstrating a steadfast work ethic until her retirement.

The small house on Dominion Street held countless cherished memories. We had some wonderful times living there. It was our home. There are a few things that I remember well. Summertime Fridays brought camping trips to Falcon Lake. Mom would have everything packed up by the time Dad got home from work, and then we'd head out onto the highway. On occasion we'd stop at the neighbourhood Dairy Queen to grab an ice cream cone to enjoy on the way.

Once we arrived at our camping spot, and while Mom and Dad got things organized, I would seize my dad's putter and a few golf balls and head over to the miniature golf course until dusk. Dad really liked to play golf at Falcon Lake. He'd be up very early on most summer Saturday mornings to play a round of golf with his buddies.

Bacon and eggs dominated our camping breakfasts, the aroma of sizzling bacon etching itself into my memories. After breakfast, Mom and Dad would clean up and we'd head to the beach for the afternoon. So much fun; I can still visualize this as I write.

On Saturday evenings after dinner, it was common for my parents to go play cards at a friend's cabin. My dad's friend from work and his family had a cabin at Block 3 in Falcon Lake. I still drive by it from time to time. Falcon Lake was more than a summer vacation spot—it would also become part of my adult life.

1972 – A Tough, Tough Year

As I've shared, growing up as a kid on Dominion Street was the best; I wouldn't trade any of it. Well, that isn't entirely true. At the outset, I said there have been some hurdles along life's way. This would be a tough one.

Mom and Dad worked hard, and my grandma (Dad's mom) lived next door. I would sleep there often, as Mom and Dad would be up early in the morning to go to work. Grandma was a very godly and caring woman. I can still remember Granny sitting on her rocking chair and singing her favourite hymns. I think her favourite was "The Sweet By and By," as she would sing it often. I can still hear Grandma singing this song and many others. I owe her an awful lot as I think back to my youth. I'd like to think she tried to plant a few good seeds in me. However, to be honest, I can't say I would recommend a family living right next door to your grandma. It can be tough on a marriage.

It's fair to say that my dad had a drinking problem. He was an alcoholic. As I remember, he sure liked his Labatt's Blue beer and Captain Morgan rum. He didn't drink every day, not at all. I suppose you could say he was a binge drinker. Dad could go days on end without drinking, or at least not abusing alcohol, but when he did drink, he'd go hard. He wasn't physically abusive to my mom or me while under the influence. As a matter of fact, my dad wouldn't tolerate any man lifting a hand to a woman. He considered that to be cowardly.

Saturdays were often the days my dad would meet his buddies at the legion or another favourite watering hole. I wouldn't see him much on Saturdays except for the summer weekends when we'd head to the lake. I think I missed something growing up. I missed a lot of time with my dad. I wish he would have come to more of my hockey games, or that we could have played some golf together. I suppose that's life. Man, I wish we could have had that time together.

There was a time when Dad's drinking did get worse, around the time I was thirteen years old in 1972. Mom gave Dad many chances, and she tried to get him to stop, or at least encouraged him to slow down his drinking. Dad tried Alcoholics Anonymous (AA) with Mom's encouragement, but it just didn't work.

As I got older, I often wondered what may have triggered my dad's drinking habit. The only thing I can think of was knowing that Dad was in a horrific motorcycle accident in 1950, when he was just twenty-two years old. He was badly busted up and close to death, as it was told to me. His injuries were far too numerous to mention, so I'll leave it at that. However, he walked with a limp his whole life after the accident. I'm told he almost lost his leg due to that accident, as the doctor at the time considered amputating. My grandpa told the doctor that if he removed the leg, my dad wouldn't want to live. By the grace of God and the work of the doctors, my dad's leg was saved.

I wonder if the trauma of that accident led to Dad's heavy drinking, at least in part. Maybe. Later on, I'll write about my work experience at Siloam Mission. I learned an awful lot about people who battle addictions like alcohol, and that often some kind of traumatic life experience leads to the addiction to try and numb the pain. During my time at Siloam, I began to think more about my dad and his addiction to alcohol.

In the fall of 1972, Mom and Dad's marriage ended. I find it very interesting that they never divorced but remained legally separated. Mom couldn't take it anymore and decided it would be best if we left. I remember coming home from school one day on a Friday afternoon and Mom was all packed up and ready to go. I don't blame her, not at all, but that was a very tough day for me, and it was extremely difficult for my mom.

The situation at home affected me. I don't like writing about this, but I did commit to being honest. My marks started to decline in school, and as I recall, one of my teachers set up a meeting with my mom to find out what was wrong with her son. I had trouble handling this situation as a youngster, and I really didn't know who to talk to. I don't think I wanted to talk about it at all with anyone anyway. As a matter of fact, I was in denial for a long time, I think all the time leading up to high school and beyond.

Whenever my friends would ask where my dad was, I'd usually say that he was working out of town or something to that effect. I lied. Why was I ashamed? This is what goes through the head of a thirteen-year-old boy, at least my head at the time.

Keeping in mind that this was over fifty years ago, there weren't many kids in my class from broken homes, maybe three or four and certainly not many more. It begs the question, "What has happened to the institution of marriage over time?" There are significantly more kids from broken homes these days. Why is that? Where is the commitment? So many questions when I was thirteen, and I have more questions today as a man in his sixties. As I look back, I believe the experience taught me a whole lot. I think this left a strong impression within me for when my day came. I wanted to do this marriage thing right. More about this later, after I fall in love!

The breakup of my parents' marriage was extremely difficult, and I wouldn't wish this on anyone. I think it leaves a scar on everyone involved. But allow me to be very clear. I do not judge my parents for this. My dad loved Mom and frankly never stopped right up until his final breath. Alcohol can abuse and destroy relationships, there is no question about it. Anyone reading this who's had a similar experience can relate. Please know that my dad would never deny the fact that his abuse of alcohol led to him losing everything of importance in his life, most importantly his marriage. I have seen and heard him admit this to his friends, co-workers, etc.

I will never forget the day my dad looked at me square in the eye when I was fifteen or sixteen while visiting him in Bow Island, Alberta. He took me to a bar for a burger and bought me a beer. I believe he thought it was my first beer. It wasn't. He looked at me, raised his glass like a toast, and said, "Do not follow my path as you make your way in life."

How hard must it be for a dad to look at his son and utter those words? I will never forget that moment. And the truth is, I have tried to follow his advice when it comes to not abusing alcohol. However, there are many of my dad's traits that I hope he's passed on to me. Dad was good natured, had a wonderful sense of humour and very few enemies, if any at all. I wish more of my friends could have met my dad. You would have loved being in his presence, and you would have laughed! Once you were "Wally's friend," you were a friend for life.

I want to say very emphatically that I have always loved my parents. Sure, I've thought from time to time what it might have been like had things worked out between them. Even now I wonder what it would be like to spend precious time together at the cabin as a family with our kids and grandchildren, and to have played some golf with dad at Falcon Lake. It just wasn't meant to be. I don't think I'm bitter about this. I just think "what if" from time to time.

And what to say about my mom? I could write pages and pages about my mom. Looking back, my mom's first priority was always me, and I mean *always*. She always put herself second. My parents' separation was very difficult for me, but it was certainly tougher for my mom—a life-changing experience.

Mom found us a place to live, and we always had a roof over our heads. Mom didn't have much money, but I never missed a meal. She worked very hard. We were close then, and we are closer now as she enjoys life today. By the grace of God, she's in her early nineties and doing well.

Upon honest reflection, I know I didn't understand as a kid all that Mom went through. I know it was a very painful and tremendously difficult decision to leave Dad, because she loved him. I believe this added to the pain for both of them because they did love each other. I hate what addiction to alcohol can do to people and their loved ones. It's an awful thing, and it can destroy so much—mainly loving and meaningful relationships.

Throughout this difficult time, Mom encouraged me to do my best in school and to stay active in sports. I know she was at ease to see that I had a solid group of friends, especially when I got involved with the youth group at church. Mom has always loved me unconditionally and consistently with her words and actions. I didn't say it nearly enough over the years, but Mom, you're the best. I've seen you laugh; I've seen you cry. And during those times when you did get upset with me, you had every reason. Oh, and by the way, Mom has a very sharp wit coupled with her strong Irish accent. I think it's safe to say I have never won an argument with her, and she knows exactly when to use that often and most reliable line, "Listen to your mother!"

Mom, I love you more than words can express. In many ways, you are my hero. Mom and Dad, I love you both.

Now, a bit more about 1972, although it's completely unrelated. I'll plant this seed now. The year 1972 was also the year when Canada beat the Russians in the epic eight-game hockey series between these two nations. If you're a hockey fan from my generation, you know exactly what I'm talking about. What in the world does this have to do with anything, and *why do I bring this up?* Well, four short years after this hockey series was over, my future wife and her family arrived in Canada from Russia. That's right, my future wife would leave Communist Russia with her family to start a new life in 1976 here in Winnipeg, although we didn't become an item for another four years. More about Helen and her family later on, just thought I'd introduce this now and tease the reader a bit. My grandma was right when she often said to me, "Jimmy, God moves in mysterious ways!"

Lord, thank you for your mysterious ways.

Passion for Sports

Growing up, my heart would beat to the rhythm of sports. The thrill of the game, the camaraderie with teammates, and lessons learned on the field were all part of my journey.

I embraced the world of organized sports from an early age, participating in school teams for soccer, volleyball, and basketball throughout elementary school and junior high. I graduated from junior high at Sargent Park in 1974. I didn't play organized school sports in senior high.

Football was my first love. The schoolyard became our playground, where friendships blossomed through our shared passions for sports and competition. I might not have been the fastest runner, but I did possess a strong arm and hands that would almost always secure a catch when the ball was thrown my way. I can also vividly recall the day I mastered the art of punting and the satisfaction of a perfectly executed spiral. In my youthful dreams, wearing the blue and gold and playing for the Bombers was a recurring fantasy. As I stated, football was my favourite sport, but the truth is, I was better at hockey than football.

Winnipeg winters ushered in a familiar ritual—throwing my skates and stick over my shoulder and heading to the neighbourhood rink. Bring back memories, anyone? Our stomping ground was the Sargent Park outdoor rink, a place of icy battles and more enduring memories. The "shack" provided solace from the biting cold, and we'd warm up by the boiler after playing for hours. Often our games on the rink would last too long and tears would mingle with laughter as our frozen feet thawed.

My formal team experiences with hockey commenced around age seven or eight, donning the red, white, and black uniform of the Sargent Park Spartans. Sharp jerseys, as I remember! I wasn't the smoothest skater, more of an "ankle bender," as they used to say. The joy of the game overshadowed any of my shortcomings. A pivotal moment arrived when I was summoned to stand in as a goalie at age nine due to a teammate's absence due to illness. Little did I know that this flukey twist of fate would define the next nine or ten years of my hockey experience.

From that game forward, I found my niche as a goaltender. The next decade saw me guard the net. I can remember thinking that I had the best seat in the house as I witnessed the ebb and flow of the game from my unique vantage point. I did manage to crack the lineup of competitive AA teams when I was fifteen years of age, but had faced the reality of being cut when I was thirteen and fourteen. That will humble you as a kid.

One of my most cherished and indelible memories emerged when my local Sargent Park community team ventured into an AAA spring tournament. This tournament, showcasing the highest level of play, was a pivotal moment for our underdog team. We were a community team, not an AAA team, but we were pretty good. We were battling through the consolation final against a team from Kenora, Ontario when I felt a buzz in the arena. During a face-off in our end of the rink, one of my teammates informed me that none other than Bobby Hull was in the stands, as his son's team was going to play after our game. Mr. Hull presented the winning trophies to our team after our victory, and his enormous handshake left an impression. He had wrists as wide as oak trees, and that deep, rusty voice that one could hear and recognize from a mile away.

I really could share more here from memories on the rink. I learned a lot of tremendous life lessons playing as a goaltender, including the true value of teamwork. Also, as a goaltender one must learn how to handle adversity and to be resilient. You also need to have a short memory, especially on those nights when the net feels very, very wide. Get the picture?

The true essence of these experiences was the relationships forged. In the world of sports, bonds transcend victories and losses. One such bond was formed with Tim Stevens, a fellow "Dominion Streeter." Our meeting at the Sargent Park shack marked the beginning of a deep friendship. Tim along with his linemates were the best players on our team. They frequently demonstrated their prowess on the ice. Tim and I spent a lot of time at the rink as well as away from it.

We did everything together. Tim's uncle was the general manager of the Winnipeg Jets back then in the early 1970s, and it seemed that every Friday night when the Jets were at home, Tim was calling me because he had free tickets. That was a blast! And in the summer, Tim and I lived at the tennis courts, and I must say we were both very good players. I spent a lot of time at Tim's house playing a lot of ping pong in his basement.

Tim's family had a cabin at a place called Laclu in Ontario, east on the Trans-Canada Highway and just before Kenora. It's a beautiful place, and Tim would invite me frequently in the summer. We would canoe, water ski, even jog sometimes. But Tim was so fast and always in better shape than me, so the jogging felt like work! These are precious memories, and as I look back, I must say how much I appreciated Tim and his family. I should add that Tim would meet his future wife, Diana, at Laclu. I had gotten to know Diana at a church youth group that I will speak about later. If one ever believed in "love at first sight," this was it.

I was honoured to have Tim as the best man at my wedding. If I was ever to be asked the definition of true friendship, I would point to Tim as an example. He is as loyal as they come. As I reflect back on the days of my youth, I could not have asked for a better friend than Tim.

Two

THE FOUNDATIONAL YEARS: HIGH SCHOOL AND A TREASURED YOUTH GROUP

ENTERING SEPTEMBER OF 1974 felt both exciting and new. Until then, I had known only one school: Sargent Park. I had a deep fondness for that school, having attended from kindergarten to grade 9. However, change was in the air—a transition was in the air—a transition to high school. New school, new friends, a new playground—it was a mix of anticipation and uncertainty. I had a plan, though. I was determined to continue playing hockey at the highest level I could achieve, and also to make my mark on the high school football team, the Daniel Mac Maroons. I think it's important to add that I also wanted to do well in school because I wanted to attend university after my high school years were done. I envisioned myself as the starting quarterback at Daniel Mac, perhaps not in grade 10, but surely by grade 11 or 12. This, as it turns out, was far from reality. My high school years took unexpected turns, guiding me through experiences that would shape my journey. I did continue to play hockey, donning the goaltender's gear for the Midland AA Flyers, the team from my district. But the football field remained elusive for me throughout high school.

    A notable incident in French class early in grade 10 marked the beginning of my musical journey. Who would have thought? The knock on the classroom door, the curious exits of my classmates—I remember being perplexed. When it was my turn, I met Mr. Barry Anderson, the revered music teacher, who would change the course of my high school years. He guided me to the music room, where my tentative singing of scales led to my inclusion in the male choir. I couldn't read a musical note for the life of me. Yes, me—a choir member. This unexpected turn set the stage for what would become one of the most transformative periods of my high school life.

The choir, led by Mr. Anderson, transitioned from male choir to include mixed choir, which meant the guys would be singing with the girls! I certainly noticed the gals; unfortunately, I'm not sure they even knew my name. Choir introduced me to more than just music. It was an avenue that led to unexpected friendships, personal growth, and valuable life lessons. In hindsight, that moment in French class marked the birth of a journey that exceeded my imagination, and that's a good thing. I was so fortunate to participate in musicals, like *Brigadoon* and *Oklahoma*, and annual performances at the Winnipeg Concert Hall. Also, I travelled with the choir to Disneyland. As a result, my high school years turned out to be defined by music and camaraderie. Mr. Anderson's unwavering guidance, patience, and challenging expectations transformed me, teaching me yet again the immense value of hard work and teamwork. When I say hard work, he pushed us and got everything out of us. These were very valuable lessons that would echo through my life's journey.

And what happened to the football dream? Remember, I had a plan! Let me try to explain.

The physical education teacher was also the football coach. I remember often in our physical education class that he would take the guys outside to teach us the fundamentals of football, and I loved it. This would ultimately result in a scrimmage. I couldn't run fast but I could throw the ball far and with velocity, so the guys would want me to be the quarterback.

One day early on in grade 10, our physical education teacher noticed that I had a very good arm, and he asked me to come out to the football team's practice. The football season had already started, but I attended "a" practice. The first thing I noticed was that neither of the quarterbacks on the team had a good arm, and they were both in grade 12. They couldn't throw a spiral if their life depended on it, and their accuracy was suspect. In my mind, they both sucked, and I was better than both of them (less than humble of me to say, but you want the truth!). I know coach wanted me to attend and watch and learn. Maybe I could be the starter in grade 11, which sounded really motivating to me.

Here comes more of the truth: the grade 12s looked ginormous to me as I saw them through my lens in grade 10. Many of them were big and certainly more muscular than me. I was about six-foot-one in grade 10 but weighed maybe 160 pounds, and that was after supper. I had no desire to get crushed and snapped in two pieces, so that one practice was the end of my high school football career. Man, that sounds so lame! In summary, I went from "quarterback wannabe" to "choir boy." Try that one on your ego when you're a young teenager. That was not the end of the story for football, though—not by a long shot. Stay tuned.

The high school years were fun. I have no regrets (well, maybe not pursuing football) and just the fondest memories. In all honesty, playing hockey and singing in the choir were great, and I managed to achieve pretty good grades too. But something much more significant took place during my high school years that shaped me for life. I'll address that next.

My high school from 1974 - 1977, Daniel McIntyre Collegiate Institute. I enjoyed 3 very memorable years here, including singing in the choir! Who knew?

By the Grace of God—A Church Youth Group

Through the choir experience at school, I eventually did meet a few of the gals in grade 10. We got to know each other better as the days wore on. I soon found out that they were very keen on their church youth group at Central Mennonite Brethren (M.B.) Church. Initially, I regarded their enthusiasm for their youth group with passive interest. Their relentless invitations finally led me to a gym night—a turning point I could never have predicted. I think I ran out of excuses and lies not to accept their invitation. They found my weakness: sports.

The gym nights were held every second Saturday evening at the Donwood Elementary School in North Kildonan. That first gym night, floor hockey turned to basketball, and camaraderie turned into genuine friendship. The warmth of this group intrigued me. There was something different about them that sparked my curiosity and admiration. By the *grace of God,* attending that first gym night turned out to be a good decision, and that's an understatement.

Young guys like to eat, and I remember they were heading to McDonald's on Henderson Highway to enjoy a Big Mac or three. They invited me, and that meant a lot, as I was just a stranger. There was something different about this group and these guys. I still remember thinking, *What is it about them?* I wasn't sure what it was, but I was curious and certainly impressed. I joined them for a hamburger, and it was a great night. This was just the beginning, literally just the beginning, as this was really a life-changer. Who knew that attending a gym night on a cold winter evening would change my life? You may think I'm exaggerating, but I'm not. It's the truth.

I mentioned that I would often find an excuse not to attend the church youth group, but after attending the gym night, something changed within me. Now I was asking when the next gym night would be, as I wanted to go. Sure, the sports activities were appealing to me, but there was more; I felt very comfortable around the guys, and I got to know them much better over the course of the next several months.

One of the first guys I met was Harold Witzke. We both had attended Sargent Park School, although he was a couple of years older than me. We established a strong bond quickly. Harold was diagnosed with multiple sclerosis as a teenager, and he battled this disease all of his adult life. He was a true friend, and we spent a lot of time together. Harold took pride in being the coach of our church football team. He was the Master of Ceremonies at my wedding. Harold passed away in 2003.

One thing led to another, and now I was being invited to attend their Bible studies. Gym nights, yes! Bible studies, no! Somehow I found myself eventually going to the Bible studies. I was attending because a group of caring friends kept encouraging me to come. Why?

Bible Studies would start with music and singing, and some of those songs have stayed with me to this day:

"It Only Takes a Spark"
"Teach Me, Lord, to Wait"
"Through It All"
"Freely, Freely"
"I've Been Redeemed"
"The Building Block"

And there are so many more.

These kids could sing Once the singing was over, there'd be an opening prayer and then our youth leader or someone else would lead the study. This was all new to me, but I found myself becoming more and more interested. There came a point when I went home and found an old Bible lying around somewhere and started to read it. I remember my grandmother on Dominion Street often talking about the Bible and the scriptures, but that was in my early youth. The more I read, the more questions I had.

Back to the youth group. I know that I sat at Bible studies as quiet as a church mouse. I had questions but was afraid to ask, until one night I asked the first one, then another, and so on and so forth. This group was so patient with me. These young people were an example of extending the love of Christ to this newcomer. People who were so influential on me were the youth leaders, including Ernie and Ursula Wiebe and then Jack and Maria Funk. They displayed such loving and meaningful leadership, and the rest of the group was very similar, as they were so loving and caring. They became friends for sure, but also mentors, guiding me through such unfamiliar spiritual terrain.

As I look back, the best way I can describe these people is as young ambassadors for Christ filling a real void in my life. Let me repeat, a *real void* in my life. I may have not understood that at that time, but it's sure clear to me now.

By the way, the food after Bible studies was unbelievable! The parents of the kids in the youth group were also special and so generous. I never left hungry; that wasn't possible. I landed wonderful friends for sure, but let's just say I learned to really appreciate Mennonite cuisine. Nice benefit!

I can't remember exactly when, but there came a time when our youth leader, Ernie Wiebe, approached me and said it was time for me to lead a Bible study. He challenged me and encouraged me. By this time, I really felt part of the group, but I was somewhat hesitant and frightened to lead a study. I'd never done this before. I was really into the Bible studies at this point. I think I was trying to contribute by reading the scriptures out loud when it was my turn and asking questions, but leading a study was going to be a giant step for me. I was still trying to learn the scriptures at this point and still very much in the infancy of my walk in getting to know who God really is. I was becoming more interested and curious every day. I don't know the topic I was given to lead, but I did it. I wish now that I had saved it. Once again, the youth of Central M.B. Church were very patient with me as I stumbled through, and they helped me when I got lost in the content or experienced difficulty as I led my first Bible study.

I am so thankful to Ernie for challenging me in such a loving and encouraging way to lead a study. The experience taught me so much, including the fact that when you prepare to lead a Bible study, you must spend time in God's Word. Yes, you spend time in the Word before a Bible study even when you're not leading, but preparation is a much different matter. You may not understand everything, or may need to read something two or three times to understand it, and there is immense value to that exercise.

When our studies were over, we'd ask everyone for prayer requests, and often many requests were shared. It was a close group, very close indeed. We bonded. And by the way, when it was time for prayer requests, I knew that the Bible study was over and I was done leading my first one! Thank you, God, that you prepared me through all my awkwardness to get through it, and thank you to all my friends in the youth group who put up with me and helped me stumble to the finish line. I must say that to this day I often think about those times, as it was such a very special time in my life.

I don't like to think what my life would have been had God not led me to this very special group.

If I didn't realize it yet, I was learning something very meaningful about life. *Relationships*—they are so important. I was learning this now, and truth be told, relationships would become central to my life. While I think of it, maybe this is a good place to enccurage everyone to find a Bible study group. I owe it to every reader to pass this on. If you belong to a church, you likely have Care Groups or Life Groups, where Bible studies happen. If you've never gone to one, that's okay. It's never too late, and there's always room for one more. If you don't attend a church, I'm hopeful you have a friend or two who might know something about Life Groups. I hope they invite you.

Our Life Group at our 2023 Christmas gathering in our home. I encourage everyone to join a Life Group. Study the bible together, talk about life together and break bread together.

A Life Group is just a small group, an extension of the church, where people can meet regularly to share God's Word, pray together, and share life. I find it to be a safe place. I'm reminded of Matthew 18:20, which reads, *"For where two or three gather in my name, there am I with them."* And by the way, Life Group gatherings almost always have good snacks and treats over coffee, and maybe even a meal together. I now see that I include the food part frequently; however, there's an argument to be made that it's biblical. There are many stories in the Bible where people break bread together.

One more thing: I must encourage parents to strongly encourage their kids to get involved with a youth group at church. The world is changing at a very rapid pace, and I think we can all agree with that statement. I only know of one constant comfort these days in a world that is searching, and it's again found in the scriptures, in Hebrews 13:8: *"Jesus Christ is the same yesterday and today and forever."* I believe that means that our God is immutable, that He is unchanging and His love endures forever for you and for me. If the last few sentences sound like a sermon, they're not meant to be. It's just my way of encouraging everyone, both young and older, to learn more about this loving God. I recall the reference to the song in my introduction: I know I am broken. We are all broken if we choose to be honest. So bring your brokenness and I'll bring mine. There is mercy waiting on the other side.

I lost my way a little bit after talking about youth Bible studies. That's okay. Remember, this is imperfect.

Central Mennonite Brethren Church on William Ave. and Juno. This church would become the foundation for my life ahead. A beautiful church in so many ways. I loved the people.

I was invited to the Central M.B. Church service one Sunday morning. I can't remember exactly when, but it was soon after I became a regular attender at youth. This was to become a very special place and it was so foundational to me as I reflect on my experiences within that church. I know I was nervous. Sure, I'd gotten to know the youth group through the gym nights and Bible studies, but this was different. There were mature adults in church! I hadn't attended church on a regular basis since I was a youngster, I would say when I was eight, nine, or maybe ten years old. I do remember reciting the Ten Commandments from memory in front of the congregation at the Harstone United Church on Sargent Avenue. I had attended Sunday school there on a regular basis, but that was really it.

The people at Central M.B. were very friendly. Notice yet again God's love at work through His believers, and it was starting to really penetrate my soul. I was the new guy in a small church with a congregation of less than two hundred. Everybody knew each other, and I was certainly the only "Bell" in attendance. After all, this was a traditional Mennonite Brethren church with recognizable surnames like Loewen, Thiessen, Funk, Wiebe, Friesen, Warkentin, Plett, Kornelsen, etc. Please note that the name "Kornelsen" would become much more meaningful in the next couple of years!

A Quick Meeting—A Lasting Impression

I remember one Sunday morning when I was still very new there. A man approached me in the small lobby at the front of the church after the service. He reached out his arm to shake my hand. I extended my hand as well, just to be polite, and he asked me, "How are you doing, young man?" Those were his exact words.

I looked at him and said, "Fine," and I kept walking past him, or so I thought. This man's hands were huge, like vice grips. The handshake would end on his terms, not mine. He looked at me square in the eye and said, "Welcome here, young man; lots of people here are praying for you." I have never forgotten that conversation; for some reason it surely meant a lot to me. This was another step, yet another real-life example of someone taking the time to reach out to someone he didn't know and to model the love of Jesus.

Central M.B. was incredibly impactful on my life, both then and now. I truly experienced what God's love is all about. I loved the people, young and old. Without Central, where would I be today? I hope you don't mind me saying it here, but another song comes to my mind. I think of a song called "The Lighthouse." The song speaks about Jesus being a lighthouse amid the storms of life. Without that lighthouse, where would I be?

The youth and members of Central M.B. Church were my lighthouse. They were the light around me, and if it weren't for them, where would Jim Bell be? I don't want to even venture a guess to that question.

Many of the relationships from Central M.B. are still alive today. By the grace of God, my life changed forever as a result of stepping foot into that church. It was my first experience with a bright lighthouse. I accepted Jesus Christ as my Lord and Saviour when I was seventeen years old. I had attended a youth event in Caronport, Saskatchewan in February 1976 called Youthquake. The speaker that night spoke right to my heart. It was there that I made my commitment to accept Jesus and to follow Him in obedience.

I was baptized at Central M.B. Church on Easter of 1981 and became very active in the church. I remember fondly my experiences as a youth leader together with my wife, Helen. I also served as a Sunday school teacher, treasurer, and on church council. Let me not forget about singing in the church choir. I gave it my best with those German songs! These were all truly wonderful things to be part of in the church, and I hope I grew in my own faith as a result. And I met my wife at Central. God is so good; He is good to me!

Please be encouraged to find yourself a church home. Everyone has a gift, whether it be practical, administrative, hospitality, musical, teaching, serving, etc. If you're reading this, please know that you have a gift. Join a church and utilize your gift to its greatest capacity and purpose. I believe you will be blessed for it.

The doors of Central M.B. Church would close permanently in 1995. This was a very sad time, and I believe everyone felt the same way. There was plenty of discussion around building a new church in a different location, or moving to a different building. It got complicated. As a congregation, we couldn't land on a unified position around this question, so everyone went their separate ways. This was difficult for everyone, regardless of whether they wanted to build, move, or stay in the same location. It was difficult because I believe the people there loved and cared for each other deeply.

I hope everyone found a church home after the doors closed at Central. I believe they did for the most part. I choose to remember all the good times at Central M.B. This church was a lighthouse that shone brightly. I trust that all of us who enjoyed family and fellowship there have continued to be a light in their churches and communities.

FALLING IN LOVE, STAYING IN LOVE

AS I'VE MENTIONED several times, Central M.B. Church profoundly changed my life. What an understatement! It was there that I met my future wife, although not right away. I had been attending the youth group for a few years, but it wasn't until the autumn of 1980 that I began to take notice of this tiny, cute, and very quiet Russian girl named Helen. Her curly hair, radiant smile, and rosy-red cheeks etched themselves into my mind. As the autumn months of 1980 rolled on, I found myself thinking of her often. To be candid, I couldn't take my eyes off her. She had no idea.

One chilly, windy evening in October 1980, our youth group organized a roller-skating outing. During the "triples skate" session, I gathered my courage and asked Helen and her friend to join me. I did this partly to avoid being alone with Helen (though I secretly wished for it). I felt somewhat guilty as I talked to Helen the entire time we skated, unintentionally neglecting her friend. My heart raced that night, and I couldn't wait to ask her for the "couples skate." She said yes, her shyness only adding to her charm. I was falling for her, but thankfully, I didn't fall on the skating rink.

Helen has reminded me that after the roller-skating event we all went out to eat together. This was a common occurrence back then after a youth event. She says she was hoping I would sit beside her, as she claims to have enjoyed my company at the rink. Like a fool, I sat with the guys.

After that memorable evening, I waited and waited before mustering the nerve to ask her out on a date. Helen and I laugh about it now; she initially thought I was interested, but my prolonged hesitation made her wonder.

Helen and I talk about our dating days from time to time. She reminds me that she thought I was interested in her when I invited her to skate couples only. However, because I procrastinated in asking her out on a date, she then thought otherwise. She was wrong! Little did she know that I couldn't sleep, my mind consumed by thoughts of her. I eagerly anticipated every youth event, Bible study, or Sunday service, wondering what it would be like to be her boyfriend.

I also remember the church's annual Christmas banquet that year. It was typically held early in December, featuring a beautiful choir program, delightful music, and a sumptuous meal. At these events I developed a true appreciation for fine Mennonite cuisine, from appetizers to desserts. And, as the saying goes, "Always leave room for dessert!" That night, Helen wore a stunning purple dress that caught my eye. I thought that sitting with her brother during the banquet would place her nearby. I was mistaken, but how could I have known? I enjoyed the meal, but my gaze remained firmly fixed on Helen. She was radiant, and I knew I had to ask her out soon.

One story from that evening stands out. I noticed Helen helping the ladies clean up after dinner in the kitchen, tackling the dishes all by herself. I saw an opportunity and walked into the kitchen. I was the sole male amidst the ladies, and I proceeded to grab a towel to help Helen. I'm sure the ladies were surprised—especially one, Mrs. Thiessen, who asked what I was doing in the kitchen. It didn't take her long to figure it out, as my face undoubtedly revealed my true intentions. I had no interest in doing dishes; my interest lay solely in Helen.

The Courage to Ask Arrives

Finally, as Christmas approached in 1980, I worked up the courage to ask her out. It happened on the front doorstep of our youth leaders' home on Moir Ave, Ernie and Ursula Wiebe. Helen mentioned that she had plans with some girlfriends that evening but suggested "maybe another time." Am I ever glad she left the door open for a future chance. So you're telling me there's a chance? I waited no more than two days before asking her again. This time, I asked her at the front entrance of Central M.B. Church, and she said yes! I had passed the first test.

Our first date took us to the Planetarium on December 27, 1980. They were hosting a Christmas show with dazzling lights and celestial wonders. It was a beautiful experience, but my nerves prevented me from fully absorbing it. I tell people that since that date, I've been seeing stars! I know it's a bit corny, but I stick with it. I also recall telling Helen that I'd pick her up at 7:00 p.m. at her home. I arrived far too early and sat in my vehicle in the Food Fare parking lot at the corner of Henderson Highway and McIvor Avenue. Helen's family lived nearby on McIvor. Waiting for half an hour feels like an eternity when nervous anticipation fills your every thought. Helen, however, was punctual and quickly joined me in the car when I arrived to pick her up. I'm sorry she had to endure a date in my 1972 Duster, a vehicle with heat only on the driver's side. But all things considered, not having heat on her side wasn't such a bad thing, especially in winter. Think about it!

Helen has told me several times that I asked a lot of questions on that date. I suppose this was me trying to get to know her better. She says she had never spoken that much in one evening in all of her nineteen years! This may because of where she came from—Russia. In a Communist country, Helen says you only spoke when someone addressed you. That was just the way. I can certainly tell you now that Helen is much more outspoken. She claims that living with me offers her no other choice.

I had Helen home early that night, and she later told me that her dad appreciated that very much. When we said goodnight, I asked her if I could pick her up the next evening. Our youth group was going skating. She agreed. She could have caught a ride with her brothers, since the rink was on the other side of the city, but I wanted to pick her up. We went skating the following evening, and as we walked in together, our presence elicited surprised looks from others—Jim and Helen, really? Yes, really.

This marked the beginning of a beautiful courtship—such a wonderful time. Dating continued, and the novelty never wore off. I couldn't wait to see her again, from the moment I dropped her off until our next meeting. Our youth group had Bible studies on Tuesday evenings, and we sat beside each other during Sunday morning church services.

Speaking of church services, I want to share the story of when Helen invited me for lunch to their home on McIvor Avenue for the first time. This took place on a Sunday immediately after our church service, about two months into our courtship. On that Sunday, I sat with Helen and her family in church. Looking out from the pulpit, the Kornelsen family would sit together on the left side of the church sanctuary, about ten rows back. There were a lot of surprised folks when they saw me sitting with the Kornelsen clan, and so nice and close to Helen. None were more surprised than our pastor, Gerhard Friesen. When he looked out from behind the pulpit and saw me with Helen, I think it threw him off a bit, but he managed to deliver his sermon very well, as he always did. Now, more about lunch at Helen's home.

It's important that I say that it didn't take long for me to see the closeness of the Kornelsen family around the table. This was very new to me in the sense that this was a family with six kids, Helen being the second oldest. I was an only child, so this was a very different family dynamic. The love and respect shown around the dining room table was quite evident to me. Helen's mom made borscht that day, and she also made these things called "roll cuchen." Hope I spelled it correctly. I had never eaten borscht, so this just added to my nerves at this first lunch. What if I didn't like it? For what it's worth, I'm not a fussy eater anyway, not at all. Well, there were no worries. I had a spoonful or two of this borscht, and it was so good. I mean delicious! And to eat the borscht with the roll cuchen, I was in my element.

I watched Dad Kornelsen and Helen's three brothers to see if they would take seconds. I surely wanted another round. And then of course there was some kind of baked dessert; it was mouthwatering. It may have been *beeninstich*! The lunch was so good, I most certainly didn't leave hungry. The most important thing I remember from that day is that Mom and Dad and Helen's siblings made me feel comfortable and at home. I left that day feeling so good about the experience. In the end, what was there to be nervous about?

Little did I know at that point that all of them would become my family one day. I am so blessed. Did God have His hand on this? I know He did. He also has a sense of humour. Nobody would have guessed that this quiet, petite Russian girl with the beautiful curly hair and cute accent would be dating this extraverted guy of Irish descent who likes to live on the edge. Well, as I said, God knew. Thank you, Lord. Grandma was right—you move in mysterious ways!

It's safe to say that I fell in love with Helen before she fell in love with me, but I had a head start. I'd had my eye on her for months before asking her out. For anyone who's experienced falling in love, you'll understand when I say that you "just know." It's hard to explain it any other way. And is there any greater feeling? The more I got to know Helen, the more I liked her, and soon enough, I loved her. It's not a stretch to say that she was all I could think about.

I can clearly recall one evening—I believe it was after a Bible study. It was likely in March of 1981, a few months into our courtship. I went home that night and was lying in my bed hoping to get a good night's sleep before heading back to university the next day. While lying there, I was thinking about Helen, and I knew I was in love with her. I needed to make a decision. Was she the one for me? If yes, then I was all in, and let the dating continue. If not, I needed to let her know. Here's what I remember: it took me two seconds to make that decision. Who was I kidding? I wanted Helen to be my life partner. I knew it after a few short months. Jim, just don't screw this up, whatever you do! So let the dating continue!

One of our favourite places to visit was Centennial Park on Raleigh in North Kildonan. One date that stands out in my memory was when I took Helen to a lovely restaurant called Trapper John's. It might have been for Valentine's Day in February 1981. Back then, it was located on St. James Street and St. Matthews Avenue in Winnipeg's west end. We went there a few times for special occasions. They offered a delightful chicken dinner with a delectable hollandaise sauce. We both really enjoyed it, but what made the night unforgettable was the dessert—an apple crumb pie served with ice cream. It was freshly made and utterly delicious. Helen later confessed that she'd never had pie with ice cream before, but she really enjoyed it. I chalked this one up as a win for me. When you're falling for a beautiful young lady, every victory counts.

It's Getting Serious

I can remember clearly the first time I held Helen's hand. In February 1981, our youth group from church went to Camp Nutimik in the Whiteshell. This was the annual winter retreat. We had some free time later on Saturday morning and decided to go for a walk. As we walked down the road by the camp, I reached out to grab her hand, and Helen obliged. It felt so good. We'd already been boyfriend and girlfriend almost two months after our first date, but holding her hand sealed the deal. From that point on, I think we always held hands when we were together, and that holds true to this day after forty-two years of marriage. It just feels right, you know.

Helen is my wife, and she's always been my girlfriend, my best friend. I think that sometimes all of us need to remember those dating days. Ask yourself what made them special, and keep those times alive. Why wouldn't we? I encourage any married person reading this to do the same. Try to keep the spark alive. Please remember that you took a vow before God. He created this beautiful institution called marriage. Let's honour it and enjoy it.

If my kids are reading this, maybe you don't want to read about the first time your parents kissed. So this is your fair warning to stop reading and skip ahead.

After about three or four dates, I admit I really wanted to kiss Helen. But did she want to be kissed by me? I can't remember where we'd gone on a date on that evening, but I decided while driving her home that I was going to kiss her. I was so scared, I didn't know how I was going to do it, but I really wanted to.

We pulled into her driveway, and just as we were saying good night, I blurted out, "Can I give you a goodnight kiss?" I'm sure it sounded awkward and clumsy, but Helen replied in her shy way with a yes. I kissed Helen good night for the first time. You know, I drove home on "cloud nine," and I just felt so good. On the way home I think I celebrated with a cheeseburger and fries from Fat Boys on Henderson Highway. Sometimes Helen and I will talk about that first kiss, and she says she thought it was so cute of me to ask. Just to finish this part of my story, on the next date I kissed her good night again, and then I snuck in a second one. Pretty selfish of me, but I'm not apologizing. I am so romantic.

Dating continued to be wonderful into the spring and summer months of 1981. There was no question we were in love. I fell hard for Helen. I knew she was the one God had chosen for me. I also remember the first time I told Helen that I loved her. I knew I loved her, and it was time she heard it from me.

We were parked on the Kornelsen driveway again, after a date. My heart was beating rapidly, and there was no stopping it. I didn't have any words planned; this was going to come straight from the heart. Well, my heart didn't prepare my mouth very well, as you'll know from my words. I looked at Helen before saying good night, and for some reason I said, "Can I say something stupid?" Just what every girl wants to here before being told "I love you"! Helen said, sure. At that point, I simply looked at her and said, "I love you."

Her gentle response with a warm smile was, "That's not stupid." She looked at me and said, "I love you too." I was so relieved that she didn't say something like "thank you" or "that's nice" or "see you in a couple of days." At first, I admit that I was crazy about her curly hair, her smile, and her rosy cheeks (the rosy cheeks are a family trait, by the way). As I got to know her, I learned that she was very quiet and didn't say a whole lot. In addition to her quiet demeanour, she has a heart of gold. She loves Jesus, loves the church, and loves her family. And thank goodness, she fell in love with me.

When Helen and I began dating, her youngest sister, Irene, was about two years old. I could see that Helen was not only a sister but also like a second mom to Irene, and she did this lovingly and willingly. I really admired this about Helen. She has always loved her family and respected her mom and dad. Often when Helen and I spoke on the phone, Helen would let me say hello to Irene. I will always remember that when Irene would say goodbye, she'd say, "I love you too you two." It was so cute, and I'm laughing as I write this. By the way, Helen and I spent a lot of time on the phone, and I know that Ed and Rita did too. There were no cell phones then, just a home landline. I apologize to Mom and Dad, because if anyone was trying to reach them, good luck!

Near the end of August 1981, Helen's family took a trip west for almost two weeks. To me, it felt more like two years! Sure, Helen would call me frequently to say hello from a payphone. I can still hear her placing the coins into the phone! Talking was great, but I missed her so very much. I knew before she left that I loved her, but if I needed any sign or convincing, her family trip was the clincher. I remember when they came home it was a Friday evening. She called to let me know they were home, and I think I got to her place in fifteen minutes, maybe less. Thank goodness there was no photo radar back then.

I don't remember when exactly we started talking about marriage, but I think it was in the spring of 1981, probably May. So we would have been dating for about four or five months. We talked about it several times as we approached summer.

Popping the Question—We're Engaged!

The Friday night when I asked to speak to Helen's parents is etched in my memory. I'm sure they had an inkling about the subject matter of our conversation. But before I delve into that memorable experience, I want to express how comfortable Helen's parents, Mom and Dad Kornelsen, made me feel in their home right from the very first lunch I shared with them. This warmth and welcome persisted throughout the years, and I must say, I love them both dearly. They embody God-loving people, serving as true ambassadors for Christ and setting a prime example of how to love and raise children. I once told Dad Kornelsen that I hold no man in higher regard than him, and I meant every word. He's a man of few words, but he exemplifies how a man of God should love his wife, family, and fellow human beings. I strive to continue learning from his example.

Now let me circle back to the matter at hand. Despite their welcoming demeanour, I couldn't help but be nervous. I hadn't rehearsed a speech or anything, but I had a clear question in my heart. We settled into their living room with Helen by my side, and there sat a bowl of fruit on the table before me. Why do I mention this? Well, I picked up a peach as I began to speak to Mom and Dad Kornelsen. It was almost a subconscious gesture, a way to channel my nervous energy. I believe I started by expressing my deep love for their daughter and my desire to spend the rest of my life with her. I promised to take care of her and then, with my heart in my throat, asked for their blessing to marry Helen. As I spoke, I inadvertently started to squeeze that poor peach in my hand. Unbeknownst to me, its juice began trickling down my arm and onto their carpet. I was completely oblivious to it, lost in the moment.

Mom and Dad Kornelsen responded with their characteristic warmth, assuring me that Helen was incredibly special to them, and they loved her deeply. They also mentioned how much they appreciated how I treated her. With their words of encouragement and affection, they gave me their wholehearted blessing to marry their beautiful daughter. I was elated. I had hoped and prayed they would say yes, and they did.

Oh, and here's a humorous tidbit. It turns out that Helen's sister Rita was quietly eavesdropping from the kitchen, listening to every word of our conversation. I didn't mind one bit; it adds a touch of charm to the story.

This is a picture of Helen and I in the fall of 1981, shortly after our engagement. We frequently talk about our dating days.

Gone Fishing

I should also mention that the very next day, I embarked on a short fishing trip with Helen's older brother, Gerhard, her sister's future husband, Ed, and our friend Walter. Our destination was a spot just past the Ontario border called Pelican Pouch, a serene locale along the Minaki Road. This outing turned out to be unforgettable, and not just because it happened the day after I got engaged.

We were in the middle of Pelican Pouch, fishing contentedly, when the ranger/inspector approached us in his boat. He requested to see our fishing licenses, to which we replied that we had left them back at our campsite. In truth, we had only Manitoba licenses, not Ontario ones. The ranger cut us some slack, instructing us to retrieve our licenses and assuring us he'd check on us later. Now, what would have been the wise course of action here? In hindsight, we should have simply returned to shore and abandoned the fishing. But in our infinite wisdom, we chose to stay in our canoe and keep fishing, even in the rain. The ranger, true to his word, returned and checked our licenses while in his boat. When we failed to produce proper permits, he issued each of us a $40 fine. He must have thought we were certifiably insane, and in that moment, he would have been correct. It wasn't my canoe, and I was merely a guest—at least that's what I told myself. What a weekend! First engaged, then a fishing trip, followed by a $40 fine, all within forty-eight hours.

The Ring

Then came the ring! I thought it would be a lovely gesture to allow Helen to choose her engagement ring. I had graduated from university a few months earlier, in the spring of 1981, which gave me an opportunity to save some money. And I knew without a shadow of a doubt that I wanted to place a ring on Helen's finger. So one Friday night, we made our way to Independent Jewellers on Notre Dame Avenue. We browsed a few options, and Helen found a ring she truly adored. I purchased it, and that moment filled me with immense pride. I had found the woman with whom I would spend the rest of my life, and we were on the verge of becoming officially engaged. During our visit to the store, we ran into a fellow church member, Herb Giesbrecht, who happened to see us. He knew precisely why we were there, and his broad smile said it all. I'm sure I looked like the cat that had swallowed the canary.

I kept the ring at home for several days after they had it properly sized. Once it was in my possession, I gazed at it daily, but I longed to see it on Helen's finger. I showed the ring to my mom, and she couldn't have been happier for us; she was also quite emotional. She'd loved Helen from the very beginning, wishing nothing but the best for her son and his future bride.

One night shortly thereafter, I went over to Helen's house and slipped the ring onto her finger. That was the moment when it became official: we were engaged to be married! The news spread like wildfire, and Pastor Friesen announced it from the church pulpit the following Sunday.

Rita, Helen's sister, was dating Ed Warkentin at the same time, another wonderful couple! They had started dating before us, and we occasionally went on double dates. They got engaged shortly after we did. I remember Pastor Friesen announcing their engagement in church a few Sundays after ours. In a lighthearted moment, he added for the congregation to pray for Mr. and Mrs. Kornelsen, as they were undergoing a "revolution" in their family. The entire church rejoiced in our happiness, and that meant the world to us. Central M.B. Church will forever hold a special place in my heart—it had to, given the extraordinary people who were part of it.

A Wedding or Two!

So let the planning begin. How were we going to do this? We both wanted to get married in the spring of 1982. We had the same circle of friends, same church, on and on. Helen tells me that it was her dad who casually said that we should consider getting married on the same day. At first this seemed kind of funny and not realistic. A double wedding? Well, the more we talked about it, the more we liked the idea, and it made a lot of sense. We agreed to do it, and now the waiting began.

We chose May 1, 1982 to be the big day. It turned out to be a beautiful day. I got up early, as I couldn't sleep. I decided to go for an early morning jog. Before I knew it, I was dressed in my black tux and getting ready for pictures. I think it was about twenty-five degrees Celsius that day without a cloud in the sky. It was a fun day, enjoyed by all. Because it was a double wedding, we decided to reduce the size of our wedding party. My best man was Tim Stevens, an easy choice. Helen's second oldest brother, Jake, also stood with me. He was so young at the time. I made a really good choice. Little did I know what the future held for Jake and me. We have had so much fun together over the years. I also chose two ushers, Bernie and Calvin, two very dear friends growing up.

Of course, there were two bridal parties, given that this was a double wedding. We all knew each other, and that just added to the fun of the day. We all attended each others' weddings back then, and it seemed like there was a wedding every second week. Where has the time gone?

Our wedding day was an absolute blast. The guest list was well over three hundred, made up of extended families, guests from Central M.B. Church, and of course our youth group and other friends. Such a memorable time. I can remember the message given during our wedding ceremony by Viktor Hamm. This man can preach, and I can remember at least in part his message to us on that day. It was based on Proverbs 25:11: "*A word fitly spoken is like apples of gold in settings of silver*" (ESV). The verse made sense then, and as I think about it, these are wise and true words for any relationship, particularly a marriage. When Viktor preached, you listened, whether it was your wedding or not.

I should also say that our wedding was held at North Kildonan M.B. Church because Central M.B. wasn't big enough to accommodate everyone we invited. Here is something to note: As Helen and I exchanged vows, I placed the ring on her finger, and then it was her turn. She grabbed my right hand, not my left! I pulled my right hand back subtly in an effort to have her place the ring on my left hand. Helen tells me that her heart skipped a beat, wondering if I was having second thoughts! Not a chance. She was wrong; placing the ring on my finger was a sign that she was going to be stuck with me for life.

One thing I will always remember is that Helen and I started our marriage with a prayer. On our first night of marriage, we got on our knees and asked God to guide us and be part of our marriage from the first day. In my heart I know that God has answered that prayer and has walked with us since Day 1. That doesn't mean that there haven't been some tough days. I think it's fair to say that every marriage has some challenging days and experiences along the way. But when those challenges arise, the key is to *work at them together with God in the centre.* Even though at times I haven't put God first or been committed in prayer, whether it be with praises to Him or in a time of need, God has been consistent and faithful. Lord, thank you for blessing Helen and I with a happy marriage. You answered our prayer on May 1, 1982 and have walked with us since. Thank you again, Lord.

Helen and I honeymooned in the Black Hills of South Dakota. It was a wonderful time and we enjoyed some beautiful scenery. We made our way home to start our life together after enjoying a wonderful week.

Four

THOSE EARLY DAYS OF OUR MARRIAGE

WE'D BEEN MARRIED about a week when we had our first … ugh, call it "misunderstanding." Helen went back to work immediately after we got back from our honeymoon. I had another week off, and on this particular day I was doing paint work and some cleaning up around our house. Helen worked at the Food Fare in McIvor Mall at the time, about five minutes away from our home. I walked into the mall, and I could see Helen working at the cashier desk. When I would pick her up from work on occasion before we got married, she always looked so happy to see me, but this day would be different. As I walked in, Helen's cheeks began to look flushed, not rosy, and her smile wasn't as radiant as I was used to seeing. We had decided beforehand that we would do some grocery shopping when Helen's shift was over. I thought things were pretty quiet as we made our way down each aisle. Before we were done, Helen said that she just wanted to go home, so we paid for our groceries and left. That's when I found out my mistake.

Helen made it very clear to me that she was not happy (understatement!) that I'd showed up in very messy and dirty paint clothes from working around the house all day. She wanted to introduce her husband to her workmates, and here I show up looking less than clean, to say the least. She was right, and hopefully I learned from it. What "broke the ice" from our first misunderstanding in our marriage was when we were unloading the groceries from our car. I picked up the watermelon and mishandled it. I lost it as it fell to the ground and splashed all over the garage floor. Have you ever had a bad day?

Our first two years of married life were so good. We both had jobs, and it seemed we always had something to do, but we certainly made time for each other. We continued to be active at Central M.B. Church. We served as youth leaders, which was an awesome time and experience. Sure, it took time and commitment, but the kids were great, and the parents were very supportive. Helen also sang in the Russian choir, and I was a Sunday school teacher. We loved Central M.B. Church and it was a pure joy to serve.

For those of you who know Helen, it won't come as a surprise to you to learn that the two things she wanted most out of marriage were to be a loving wife and mother. I can speak to both of these. Simply put, she was born to do both. Helen was born to love and be loved. Ask our kids how they feel about their mother. They love her, respect her, protect her ... get the picture?

Kids!

Speaking of kids, Helen wanted to be a mom before I wanted to be a dad. Maybe it wasn't so much about "wanting." I was just a bit reluctant and maybe scared. Why? I think in part it was because I didn't have a proper father-son relationship with my dad as I grew up. I didn't feel totally equipped to be the dad I wanted to be once the time came. Does this make any sense? And please don't get me wrong—it's not because my dad didn't love me or that I didn't love him. Nothing could be further from the truth. I know my dad loved me. Dad's alcohol got in the way of a lot of stuff in our house. Sure, I wish I would have had more teaching and mentoring moments from Dad. But I loved him right to his last day.

Back to having kids. A big moment came in the fall of 1984. I came home from being on the road in Dauphin for a week for work. I'd been eating in restaurants all week and sleeping in a strange hotel bed. I was looking forward to getting home to my wife, my own bed, and a home-cooked meal. I walked in the door on a Friday afternoon. After greeting me with a hug and kiss, Helen asked if we could go out for dinner. *Really, Helen? I've been eating in restaurants all week.* I just wanted to stay home, but I didn't put up any fuss at all and said, "Sure, where do you want to go?"

We had a coupon book, and we ended up going to this very nice restaurant called Kennedy's. It was on the twelfth floor or so, where the Radisson Hotel is currently on Portage Avenue. It was really nice, quite elegant. The food was delicious, and the atmosphere was top-shelf, as well with a piano player. Before we ordered our meal, Helen looked at me and said, "Do you remember what I wanted for last Christmas?" Last Christmas! I can never remember things like that, but I made a few guesses. I think Helen gave me a couple of clues before she responded with something like, "I thought I said I wanted a baby." She smiled at me so proudly and said, "I'm pregnant." She was simply beaming. Well, I do remember that night very clearly as well as my immediate reaction. I know I started to cry, told strangers sitting at tables close by, phoned my mom … I'm not sure I could feel my feet under me.

On July 23, 1985, our first child was born: Trevor James Wally Bell. I'll tell you more about him later. I mentioned earlier that I was nervous about becoming a father. But when you hold that eight-pound-two-ounce gift from God the first time, the nerves are overtaken by joy, incredible joy. Now I couldn't wait to get him home. I was a dad. And I wanted to be the best dad possible to little Trevor and his siblings who would follow. Helen and I knew that we wanted more than one child. We had originally spoken about having four of these little rugrats. Trevor would need a playmate, so we obliged him.

Similar to Trevor's announcement, Helen made it special when she let me know she was pregnant again. She prepared a nice romantic evening at home and then told me that we would be parents again. I was thrilled! Helen was due with baby number two in early August 1987. We were thrilled and couldn't wait to give Trevor a sibling. And Helen absolutely loved being pregnant with each of our kids—a natural-born mom.

As we got closer to the August due date, we would sometimes joke about the possibility of our second-born arriving on my birthday, July 28. We both remember that when Helen went into labour with Trevor, I teased her about waiting another five days so he could be born on my birthday. Sure, that would be cool, and I said to Helen that maybe this time she could get it right. Remember, I was kidding!

I remember Helen and I bedding down on the eve of July 27, about two weeks before her due date. It was just past midnight when Helen tapped me on the shoulder to wake me up and inform me that she thought she was in labour. She told me it may be time to go to the hospital. So she was telling me just after midnight when the calendar had turned to July 28, my birthday. It was then that I may have said the stupidest thing a husband could say to his pregnant wife as she was experiencing contractions: "Go back to sleep; it's in your head." Yep, I said it. This was a classic case of "foot-in-mouth disease" demonstrated by me. It wasn't the only time I said something I wish I could take back; however, this may have been the dumbest. I'm embarrassed as I write this, but I have to be honest, right?

About two hours later, Helen tapped me on the shoulder again and said, "It's not in my head." We went to St. Boniface Hospital (by the way, all three of our kids were born there), and Helen was checked by a nurse. The nurse said to Helen that she was going nowhere, as the baby would be born soon. I would again pay the price for my bonehead "it's in your head" comment, as Helen looked at me in front of the nurse and said, "See, it's not in my head." Well, the nurse let me have it once she knew the whole story. I had no response and took my own advice to just keep my mouth shut.

The wee hours of July 28, 1987 were very hot. The day definitely got into the mid-thirties Celsius, as I recall. During the middle of the night as we awaited the arrival of our second child, there was a light show in the sky. Then came the moment when Helen gave birth to our second son, Cory Jake Bell. Another gift and blessing from God above. And I was so proud to have another son born on my birthday. After the delivery, Helen's first words to me were, "Happy birthday! This gift couldn't be any more personal. I love you." I didn't have the words then or now to describe hearing her say that after a long, hard labour. I think I have to say to all men that we have it very easy when it comes to the arrival of babies. Anyone disagree?

Here's another memory from Cory's birth. I brought Trevor (two years old) up to the hospital to meet his little brother for the first time. Trevor was curious to be sure, but he did something we will never forget. All you parents know that babies and little ones like their security blankets, and Trevor was no different. And he did not share his with anybody—until he met his brother Cory. I think we still have a VHS tape somewhere that shows Trev placing his own blanket on his brother, and very gently at that. Immediately, Trev was playing the role of big brother and showing Cory some love. He should have stopped there, however, as he also took Cory's new soother, stuck it in his own mouth to clean it, and then tried to really jam it into Cory's mouth. Cory had received a mixed message from big bro. Like Trevor, I will tell you more about Cory later.

Having two sons to come home to was just awesome. I can remember very clearly driving home after work and pulling into the driveway. There they were, Trevor and Cory, standing at the front window waiting for me to come home. That picture is etched in my mind. Where did the time go? We would play, of course. We'd often wrestle, and they'd gang up on me. When they were old enough, I'd put them in the seat on the back of my bike and take them for bike rides through the park. They both loved it. Bedtime was also a memorable time when the boys were small. I can remember reading them Bible stories from a red *Children's Bible*. Trevor and Cory loved it. I can still hear their sweet voices making the animal noises when I would read the story of Noah's Ark. Precious memories for sure.

As I mentioned previously, Helen and I initially desired to have four children. Before you have four, you need to have three. In the middle of January 1990, I got a very personal invitation from Helen. It stated that she and the boys would pick me up after work and we would have a "family date." To my surprise, Helen had packed a suitcase and had made a reservation to stay overnight at the Delta Hotel. It sure sounded like a great idea, but what was the occasion?

After we checked into our room, Helen had a present for all three of us— Trevor, Cory, and me! The boys each got a small micro plane. They were very popular at the time, and the boys loved them. Now it was my turn. I opened my gift, and to my surprise it was a tiny, little pink dress. I had no idea how to react. I was clueless. Helen had to explain it me, as usual. She went on to tell me that baby number three was on the way, and she was hoping this time would be a girl. That explained the dress.

Helen had also made arrangements for dinner, so I needed to take a shower and get cleaned up. In my excitement, I overlooked one thing: I had forgotten to place the shower curtain inside the tub. The result was not good as I proceeded to flood the bathroom floor. Oh well, what's one more absent-minded moment?

Fast forward to September 7, 1990. It was 7:00 p.m. on a Friday evening when our nine-pound-six-ounce bundle of joy was born, our third child! As it turned out, the tiny pink dress was an appropriate gift, as Helen gave birth to our beautiful little girl, Acksanna Courtney. While growing up in the

'70s in Russia, Helen says the name Acksanna was a very popular one. Helen always loved that name, so we chose that for our daughter.

Helen experienced some complications after the birth of Acksanna, and her whole family chipped in to help us for the next few weeks. We really appreciated this. Although we had intended on four children, upon the advice of Helen's doctor, we decided not have any more children. So three it was!

I can't help but think back in time as I write this piece. Trevor, Cory, and Acksanna have brought me so much joy in my life. I can't possibly write and capture all those precious times in a few short paragraphs. The truth be told, they certainly challenged me as a dad as they grew up. Sometimes it was just one of them, and sometimes they were guilty together as a unit. It's all good. I loved those days when they were small and as they grew up to become teenagers and then adults. They were my kids then and they're my kids now. I love them dearly.

Here they are! Trevor (5), Acksanna (2 or 3 months).and Cory (3). Those were good days.

Our kids are a little older here, clowning around while we were on vacation. I cherish the memories watching them grow up, and being dad. I loved them then, love them even more now.

This is our last family vacation as just the five of us, in Cuba, 2006. They grew up so fast!

Five

THE COTTAGE—OUR LITTLE PIECE OF HEAVEN

ALLOW ME TO set the stage. As of now, I've penned many of the other chapters of this endeavour, but it would be remiss not to include a chapter about our haven at 4 Par Bay, Falcon Lake. As I sit at the kitchen table in our cottage on this Sunday afternoon, August 13, 2023, to compose this, there couldn't be a more fitting moment to delve into the significance of our cottage—a place where tranquility reigns and life takes on a gentler pace. I don't take this retreat for granted. I revel in the silence and solitude; it's a balm for the soul. I feel genuinely at peace.

You've glimpsed into my formative years spent with my parents and, later, the chapter with Helen and our children. There's a common thread weaving through both these phases: our camping escapades at Falcon Lake. What follows is an extension of those cherished moments.

Helen and I spent a decade camping with our children at a seasonal site at Falcon. These were cherished times spent first in our fourteen-foot Travelaire trailer, followed by a bigger pop-up tent trailer. The memories etched during that period are indelible. However, as the kids grew and immersed themselves in their own pursuits, like their sports tournaments, we reached a juncture where we couldn't be in two places at once. Thus, the era of seasonal camping had to end.

Several years elapsed before Helen and I felt the itch to seek out a cottage. We looked in many places throughout the province, and Falcon Lake, with its enduring allure, was part of our quest. After a few years of searching, we stumbled upon our idyllic retreat—4 Par Bay. To make a long story short, in the spring of 2009, we took a day trip to Falcon to check out a cabin at the advice of a friend. We were so disappointed as we toured this place. As we left, we decided to go for a drive, and Helen spotted a "for sale" sign on another cottage property. We stopped to have a closer look. No one was there.

Helen had me lift her up so she could have a better look inside the front window. I'm sure the neighbours were impressed! I looked like a prowler, and in broad daylight. Well, we called the agent and proceeded to have a long look inside. The rest is history! We acquired the cottage in July 2009, right around the time of my fiftieth birthday. Subsequently, we undertook renovations, adding a couple of bedrooms, refurbishing the bathroom, and adorning the interior with pine. We also equipped it for winter, discovering Falcon's unique charm in the colder months. This cherished place has now become a significant part of our lives, a place we share with our loved ones and dear friends.

At the cottage, we aim to offer a welcoming embrace to everyone. But to be candid, we also relish our solitary moments here. A typical summer weekend sees us setting out on Highway #1, eastward-bound, later on a Friday afternoon. The journey, a mere ninety-minute drive from our Winnipeg residence, unfolds along a divided highway—effortless and picturesque. We arrive, unpack, and surrender ourselves to the weekend or our summer break.

The cottage has become a crucible for cherished traditions. Laughter pervades as we engage in card games, with dominos often claiming the Saturday evening spotlight. Ah, Saturday evenings! More often than not, we venture to the ice cream parlour with family and friends, or just the two of us. It's no more than a ten-minute stroll away. Helen's preference never wavers; it's a vanilla cone, dipped in coconut, served in a bowl. That, they say, is the path to her heart. While Helen and I relish our moments at the beach, they've dwindled compared to the years when our children were young. That's just fine; we continue to appreciate it. However, the warm summer sun has an uncanny knack for sapping my energy quicker these days.

For me, the ultimate retreat is a solitary walk by the lake. Helen and I often stroll together before I embark on a brisk solo jaunt. There's a therapeutic quality to these walks. Have you ever combined walking and prayer?

Often I invite Jesus to accompany me, setting my pace. I walk, I pray, and I endeavour to soak in the beauty of His creation. It's a calming and rejuvenating experience. I invite you to try this, just you and Him. I think Jesus did lots of walking, so I know He s up for it.

But let's not lose sight of the fact that the cabin, in essence, is just four walls. Its charm derives not merely from its physical attributes but from the tapestry of relationships woven within its confines. I pray that more memories are yet to be etched into its walls, augmenting our cherished traditions. Should you ever find yourself in the vicinity, do drop by. The coffee is invariably brewing, and Helen usually bakes a treat or two for our time at the cottage. Ah, baking—a delightful tradition that I savour in this cabin. Careful, though, if you drop by on a Saturday night. Helen is a competitive dominos player!

Our cottage at Falcon Lake, a place of peace, solitude and fun! Helen and I love our time here together with family, friends and also spending time alone.

A PASSION FOR THE GAME

AS NOTED EARLIER, football was my favourite sport growing up, and it all started in the schoolyard. I played one or two years of six-man tackle football at Orioles Community Club when I was eleven or twelve. It was fun, but we certainly weren't a very good team. I think we won one or two games each year while driving our coaches crazy in the process.

I need to fast forward to 1978 or 1979 when I was twenty years old. A young guy at the time by the name of Garth Klassen started the Winnipeg Church Flag Football League. The "original six" church teams were from Portage Avenue Mennonite Brethren (M.B.) Church, River East M.B., Grant Memorial Baptist, McDermot Avenue Baptist, Calvary Temple, and us, Central M.B. Church.

As it turned out, Garth had a great idea. The calibre of football was very competitive, as you can imagine. The league started as "seven-on-seven," and although it was flag football, it was full contact, with blocking, running plays, physical play, etc. There were certainly lots of bumps and bruises, and I'm shocked there weren't more serious injuries. Perhaps a guardian angel was in attendance at all these games. One thing I will always remember is that the games would end with teams congregating at centre field to pray together after beating on each other for two hours.

After a few years, Garth was planning on stepping down as president of the league, and he asked me if I'd consider taking it over. I agreed to do so. It was a real honour. I suppose it was an initial test of my leadership skills as well. I enjoyed doing it because I had such a passion for the game. The league lasted for ten years or so, although I had stopped playing a few years before it wound up. It was fun—loads of fun. Our team from Central M.B. managed to win one championship, but looking back, the most important thing was the friendships. Many of the young men I met way back then have become friends, forming long-lasting friendships and relationships that I value today. These friendships were born out of that football league. Sure, I butted heads with a lot of these guys back when we were young and full of energy, but I value the friendships. It's about people and meaningful, long-lasting relationships. When my days wrapped up playing in this league, I thought that was it. Thanks for the memories, as they say. I was wrong. Read on.

More Football—Just the Beginning

In the fall of 1989, I saw an ad in the *Winnipeg Free Press* for an autumn touch football league. This was part of the Winnipeg Touch Football League. I thought it would be fun, so I asked a bunch of guys if they'd like to play. Something to do and enjoy in the outdoors during the beautiful fall season. I thought this would be a "one time" thing. Well, I entered a team, and who knew what this would lead to? I think it's fair to say that answering this ad would have a profound impact on my life and the lives of many others.

The team was made up of my brothers-in-law (Jake and Henry) as well as a bunch of guys we'd played against in the previous church league. The names include Perry Loewen, Garth Klassen, John Schmidt, Rob Kessler, Gord Neudorf, and Bram Bergen. There are more, but I just can't recall all the names. We won the championship for this fall league. Again, this was just the beginning. It was the start of something very special for many reasons. And it's still going today!

We decided to enter a team into the Winnipeg Touch Football League (WTFL) for the 1990 season, the year following our very successful autumn season. We did extremely well in the 1989 fall league, so why not? Our team entered the 1st Division, which is highly competitive. Our team's name was the "Eagles," and that remained for close to thirty years. Henry Kornelsen, my brother-in-law, came up with this team name. I'm not sure how he came up with the Eagles, but I always liked it. The name was appropriate.

There was one division higher, called "Elite," and this was the "creme de la crème." Two highlights come to mind from our initial 1990 season. We finished the regular season with fifteen wins, two losses, and one draw, which was very good. We went on to win another championship. That's two in two years! The first time we played the number-one elite team in the province, we beat them, which really had the league talking.

We were very proud of our accomplishments in our first full season, so much so that we just kept playing, season after season. There's no question that I could write a book containing all the fabulous memories and many accomplishments of the Eagles over the years. It all started in 1989, and this team is still alive today in 2024. These days we call ourselves the "Knights," and again the team's name was chosen by my brother-in-law Henry. We have also had the pleasure of joining with a bunch of awesome young men to form a team called the Menno Knights. We are grateful to have met and enjoyed playing the game with them.

Many of the faces have changed but there remains a core group that I will talk about later. The men I've played with over all these years should know that I really appreciate them. I was privileged to play with a lot of very talented guys, but more importantly, they helped define the character of the team, the Eagles. We weren't perfect by any stretch of the imagination; however, I must say these men defined the true meaning of "team." These teams were loaded with men of sound character. I will always appreciate their athletic abilities, but I most respect their personal attributes. I truly believe playing ball with these guys made me a better person. I want to thank them from the bottom of my heart for their contributions to the Eagles. You're all part of the Eagles family. This extends to your wives and families as well—such an awesome group of people.

From a competitive standpoint, we've enjoyed many successes over the years on the field. In the WTFL, we won three Elite championships and three Division 1 titles. We moved on to play in a couple of other leagues, including one called the PIT. We've won numerous championships, including in the indoor league. When you're fortunate to play with talented guys who demonstrate teamwork and camaraderie like this bunch, you're going to have your share of successes and accomplishments ... together.

I can't write about the Eagles and not include our travel experiences. We were very fortunate to have travelled down the highway to Regina to play in the annual Labour Day Tournament each year in September. If my memory serves me correctly, I believe we started travelling to this tourney in 1992, and it became an annual journey and so much fun. Many of us would bring our families, and in the early years our kids were small. We'd get a hotel with a waterslide, and everybody enjoyed themselves. We grew close—very close. We travelled together, stayed in the same hotel, and enjoyed meals together. Our friendships simply grew over the years because of trips like this. The Eagles personified "team," and this is what I'm most proud of. We went to play football; however, the family and friendship piece was every bit as important. The bond between us grew deeper over time. I love my teammates and their families. They are so incredibly special to me to this day.

Speaking of travelling, as our team evolved and got better competitively, we decided to travel to the annual National Tournament of Champions. This tournament is a national championship where the best teams in the country play on Thanksgiving weekend. The tournament is held most often in eastern Canada. We've travelled many times to Ottawa, Montreal, Toronto, and Hamilton to compete. The level of competition is stellar; every team is very good, and the tournament is so well organized. First class! I would call it the Super Bowl of touch football. We've done very well there over the years and have come home after winning a couple of divisional championships. We were never the best team in the country, but we always played hard and well. I know our team has always been well respected. The last time we attended this tournament was 2016, and we won the consolation championship. (As I write this piece, we are currently planning to travel again to Brampton, Ontario in early October 2022 to compete again. Our families will join us. Note: The trip to Brampton took place before the completion of this memoir. More to follow later on.)

The Core

I made mention of the "core" guys who have been Eagles and Knights for thirty-five years. The four who remain are my brothers-in law, Jake and Henry Kornelsen, and our dear friend Sean Lehmann. I say dear friend, but Jake, Henry, and I all consider Sean to be a brother. Let me try to briefly describe these guys in a few different ways. I'll start with their abilities on the field and then tell you about their character.

Jake is simply a very talented player, pure and simple. To this very day, he catches almost every ball thrown his way. Keep in mind he's now sixty years old, not a youngster anymore. Look at the size of his hands and you'll understand why—they make a football look the size of a tomato. I was always the quarterback, and when our team needed a big play, I'd most often look his way.

Over the years, our signature play was called the "in." It's not complicated. For all you football fans, Jake would simply line up wide on the left or ride side of the field and run a hard slant into the middle of the field. The play had some variations in terms of how short or long the "in" was in terms of yardage, along with a few other intricacies. In the end, it was simply "the in." Try covering Jake on an "in route" if you're a defender. He's tough, fearless, and determined, and he'll go through a wall to catch a ball for the team. I watched so many guys try to cover him. The play wasn't always successful, but it was the vast majority of the time, like 90 per cent of the time. He often left players in his wake as he went to catch the ball, even if the defender knew it was coming. He is the dream receiver for a quarterback!

I think it's safe to say that Jake and I had a tremendous chemistry on the field. That's going to happen when you play together for close to forty years, when you include the Church League. One last comment: Sometimes my teammates would get frustrated with me for throwing Jake that "in" pass when he had two or even three guys defending him. It didn't matter to me, as I knew there was a very good chance he was going to catch the ball. I had so much confidence in him. He's the kind of guy and player who will put the team on his back. He's that way in life too.

And then there's Henry, Jake's younger brother. He's cut from the same cloth in so many ways. He knows only one way to play, and that's hard—100 per cent on every play. From a physical standpoint, he's certainly different than his brother, Jake. Henry is a bit slimmer and lighter but still tough in his own right.

In the early years, Henry took over leading the Eagles' defence as captain, and he did it well. He always seemed to put guys in position to make plays. That's one of his characteristics as a leader, helping others to succeed. I think he took a lot of pride in leading our "D," and he was good at it. I know he always had the respect of his teammates. Henry would also play on offense, especially in the younger years. I'm not sure he ever came off the field back then. He had those sure hands, and whatever I threw to him, he caught.

I remember one play in particular; I call it the "passing of the torch." We were playing in the Labour Day Tournament in Regina in a semifinal game against a team from Winnipeg called the Ratz. They were a very tough and well-respected rival of the Eagles. They were an excellent team, loaded with talent. We hadn't beaten them back home, but we were getting closer, and we felt it was just a matter of time. In this particular game, it was going back and forth. We went ahead with about three minutes left in the game and we were excited, but we needed a stop from our defence. We'd put it in the hands of our captain on D, Henry. Well, as I remember, we were watching from the sidelines, and Henry was covering one of the Ratz's main players. Their quarterback threw the ball to this guy, and Henry jumped in front of it, intercepted the ball, and ran it all the way back for a long touchdown. Game over! That was a big moment in the young history of the Eagles. This was the "passing of the torch." I believe from that point on we beat the Ratz often. Henry's big play was paramount and so memorable.

And then there's Sean. Sean was not an original Eagle. We'd play against him from time to time in our early years as the Eagles. We took note of him for two reasons. For one, he was extremely fast and a very good player. And two, he wore red sweatpants, so he stood out. We didn't know his name, so we always referred to him as "red sweats guy." It was a form of respect, as he did stand out on his team.

As I recall, Sean approached me one winter night in the early 1990s as we were both playing on separate teams. We were playing in the indoor winter league at the Golf Dome on Taylor Avenue. He was very respectful and expressed his sincere interest in joining our team. I talked it over with Henry, and we invited him to join. It was a great decision for several reasons. I can remember Sean's first game with us. On the first play of the game, we received the kickoff, and the ball was kicked to Sean. He returned it all the way for a touchdown. That's quite a feat in touch football, considering all you have to do is touch a player for a play to end. Sean avoided being tagged by everyone in his path. I think he was wearing those red sweats too—so appropriate!

What an acquisition! He made me look good for recruiting him, but the truth is that he approached me. Sean went on to be a pillar on our team, yet another example and definition of a true teammate. He also had a signature play like Jake, but Sean's play was the "up and over." In simple terms, he'd line up on the left side of the field and run up and across the field, making his way down the field very fast, and I mean fast!

Once Sean made his break across the field, I would generally throw him the ball and try to lead him so he could run under it. It was a money play! Once Sean got behind you, he was gone. "Red sweats guy" was not going to be caught. Sean fit into our team immediately and perfectly as I think about it.

"The "core" of the Eagles and Knights for over 30 years. (from left to right, Jake Kornelsen, me, Sean Lehmann, and Henry Kornelsen). I cherish the memories and experiences with these three men.

Shared Qualities, Shared Legacy

In summary, Jake, Henry, and Sean have different physical gifts and attributes on the field. They have all demonstrated their talents over many years, going back to 1989. They are pillars and cornerstones of our team and in my life. I must point out their similarities as well. They have always been leaders on the field and respected by their teammates and opposing players. They give it their all for the team, not for themselves.

They are examples and role models, and they define trust, integrity, and men of character. Most importantly, they love their wives and families. These are guys you want on the field on your side to try and win a game. More importantly, these are men you want by your side in life during the good times as well as the challenging ones. As the quarterback of the team, I've thrown many interceptions over the years. During those times when I struggled, they were the ones who encouraged me to keep going. And to be honest, they would get after me a bit too. In life they are the same. How good has it been for me to have these three men of character beside me both on the field and off? They hold me accountable. I appreciate them so very much, and it's time to tell them. I love these men and cherish their friendships. We were the Eagles on the field. I think it's fair to humbly say that we flew high together, and I thank them for allowing me to latch on to their wings and enjoy the ride. Henry, maybe you knew something when you came up with the team's name, Eagles.

It wouldn't be right if I didn't say something about their families. Our team was always a close bunch. As I mentioned, we travelled together to countless tournaments and enjoyed many good times together. I can't mention them all by name, but they need to know I appreciate them all. It was a privilege to have you all part of the Eagles and Knights family. A few deserve special mention. To Monica, Laura, and Geni, I thank you personally for allowing your husbands out of the house to play ball. Helen, thank you as well for allowing me to try and stay young by playing ball with my buddies. All four of you have always been there as our loyal "season ticket holders" and faithful fans. You've always been the Eaglets and the Ladies. In case you don't know, the wife of a Knight is known as a "Lady." You're a very special group of women—certainly special to me. How many good times have we shared together? I hope there will be many, many more.

I also thank the Kornelsen and Lehmann families for allowing me the absolute privilege of playing with their sons. Their names are Jeremy, Owen, Jordan, and Keenan. I know I can say they are following in the footsteps of their dads in many ways. And a word to you four boys: I have enjoyed every minute playing with you! In addition, I want to express my gratitude to Chris Dyck, yet another class act who has contributed in so may ways to our team. And to Trevor, my son: It was my absolute privilege to be in the huddle with you and to throw you many balls.

Seven

A TOUCH FOOTBALL ODYSSEY: RESILIENCE, TEAMWORK, AND TRIUMPH

> "If you want to go fast, go alone. If you want to go far, go together" (African proverb).

THIS CHAPTER WAS never even a thought. Not for a second did I think I would be adding it. I need to circle back and include this experience. It's far too meaningful to leave out. I'll do my best to describe what I was so proud to experience with a group of men.

The Last Dance

In the spring of 2022, our Knights team discussed the possibility and then decided to travel one more time to the Canadian Touch Football Tournament of Champions. This would be held in Brampton, Ontario in October on Thanksgiving weekend. As we made the decision to do this one more time, I had some legitimate concerns and feelings of trepidation. *Are we too old? Can we really expect to compete at such a high level again? Can we get enough players to commit to making the trip?* There were more questions, and these were legitimate concerns. I must say I had one very real concern of my own. I had shared with my wife, Helen, a few times leading up to this trip that I did not want to embarrass myself. I certainly didn't want to let the team down. The passion to play with my teammates at this level still burned within me; however, I was concerned about my age and declining abilities.

I'll fast forward to August 2022, when we put our team together consisting of seven players from our Knights team and seven more from a team we often competed against in our league. They were a good team and a bunch of good guys. We knew them quite well. But could we make this work? How would this group get along, let alone compete? Can we develop the right team chemistry very quickly that would be necessary to compete at a high level?

We held one practice—only one! This was held one week before travelling to Brampton. I must be honest when I say that the practice did not go that well. We made several mistakes. I know I certainly did. After all, we were only getting to know each other as teammates.

Many of the teams we'd be facing were well-oiled machines, as they'd played together all year and beyond. Our team gelled immediately, and we grew closer as the tournament went on. We shared breakfasts and dinners together, and even some pumpkin and pecan pies one night in the hotel. After all, it was Thanksgiving. We got to know each other better personally as the weekend went on. I could sense that we were bonding on and off the field as the weekend progressed. This bonding would translate into success.

Our touch football team, the Knights. Together, we won the BB National Championship in October, 2022 in Brampton, Ont. What a team! I will never forget that weekend.

Game Time

I want to briefly tell you about the games we played and our journey through this championship tournament. Saturday morning, October 8, 2022, arrived, and game one was scheduled to begin at 10:15 a.m. I think it's fair to say that there were some nerves as we took to the field; however, it didn't take long for me to see that every member of the team was "all in" and there to do their very best to help the team win. This became a central theme in my eyes throughout the weekend. It was all about "team," and with that mentality, let the results take care of themselves as far as I'm concerned. I don't think anybody ever wavered from this. There were times when our character was tested—severely tested, in fact. We all knew there would be many times when we'd face adversity. Sounds like life, come to think about it. How would we respond?

It would be so easy for me to provide details about every game we played in the Tournament of Champions, and perhaps I will one day, but not here. I'll provide a summary, though. The Knights went undefeated in their tournament draw with three wins and zero losses (3-0) in our pool before entering the playoff round. Things would only get tougher. I think we surprised ourselves with our very successful start; however, we worked so hard together as a team. Please understand that this tournament is made up of the best teams from across the country, mainly from Ontario.

Now to the playoff round. We won our first three playoff games before playing the championship final. This was quite an accomplishment. We had won six games in a row. None of us could have imagined this. Playing in the championship game would mean playing seven games in three days, including three on the final day, Monday. We were tired mentally and beat up physically, but we were so excited to reach the championship game.

Before playing the championship game, we had to win a semi-final match. To make this more intriguing, we would have to play a rival team from Winnipeg. We got down in this game by two touchdowns, but our team rallied and found a way to overcome the adversity to win 13-12. As this game went on, I couldn't help but observe my teammates and their attitudes when our backs were against the wall. The only way to describe it is to say that we won because "team" was more important than "self" to all fourteen guys. This mentality would be needed and was also demonstrated a couple of hours later.

Our Touch Football Super Bowl

Now on to the championship game. We didn't expect to be there. Sure, we'd won six games in a row, but now was the real acid test. Our opposition was a team from Montreal, a young and athletic group, but I must say every player there throughout the weekend looked young to me! We didn't get off to a great start in this game; maybe we were running out of gas. Things were not looking too good for the Knights as we trailed 12-0 heading into the fourth quarter, down to our last fifteen minutes.

Once again, though, everyone dug down real deep, and our team found an extra gear as we came back to win 13-12. It was a nail-biter for sure. We won the game with our final score with twelve seconds remaining in the game. Maybe it's easy for me to say this next part now because we won; however, I do remember that there was a collective peace and calm in our huddle as we moved the ball down the field together to score the tying touchdown. I sensed that everyone was going to do whatever had to be done. There was no hint of panic, just an attitude of "let's go do this."

It Just Felt So Good

I've played competitive touch football for over forty years, and I can say that I've never experienced anything quite like this championship weekend in Brampton. The feeling of accomplishment after the final whistle blew was surreal and hard for me to explain. The guys looked exhausted; I know I certainly was. A full gambit of emotions was evident as we celebrated on the sidelines with our championship trophy and team jackets. I know I had tears flowing down my cheeks. I tried to freeze the picture in my mind, as this was a precious memory. I must say that it was my absolute privilege to play with these men. Winning was awesome, a euphoric feeling for sure. I could see this on the faces of all my teammates. I was overjoyed for them, as they had bonded and played their tails off over the course of three days.

More Important than Winning

As I reflect on this experience, I believe that something more important than winning has become apparent to me. My teammates demonstrated at least three critical traits over the course of this very special weekend. These traits include resiliency, perseverance, and character, and they are certainly needed to win a championship. More importantly, they're needed in life. Some might say it was just a game. I say it was a life lesson and that yet again relationships are at the centre. When people work together, support one another, and trust one another, you can accomplish great things together.

Put the team's interests ahead of your own and it can be a beautiful outcome. I was the oldest guy on the team, as we ranged in age from eighteen to sixty-three. This is just one of the many things about this team that makes it so unique and special. I mention that I'm the oldest because one is never too old to learn. I learned from my teammates over the course of these three unforgettable days. What did I learn? That there are incredible synergies to be gained by true teamwork, and I discovered the rewards of resiliency, perseverance, and character. Yes, we won the championship at this tournament, and I will always cherish the accomplishment. However, the friendships that grew throughout those three days will stay with me forever. I respect and value my friendships with all the guys on this team, the Knights.

I Am a Packers Fan

From an early age, I've been a dedicated football fan, and by now you've probably picked up on that. I've already shared my childhood dreams of becoming a Winnipeg Blue Bomber, a dream shared by countless kids in our schoolyard. But there's more to my football fandom than just the Blue Bombers. Somewhere along the way, I became a passionate fan of the Green Bay Packers.

My first memory of the "Pack" dates back to 1967 when I was just eight years old. I recall watching them on our black and white television, battling the Dallas Cowboys in what would become one of the most legendary games in NFL history: the "Ice Bowl." It was a frigid encounter. I think I shivered in front of the TV as I saw the breath of the players leave their helmets. I believe it was on that day that I unknowingly cemented my loyalty to the Packers.

A Special Place

A little bit about Lambeau Field and Green Bay, Wisconsin. Green Bay is a relatively small city. As you enter the city limits from the highway, you'll see a sign that reads, "Green Bay, Population of 102,000." That may not sound like a big deal, but how does a city that small have a franchise in the National Football League? And this small city has a football stadium that seats eighty thousand or so. I think the biggest building I saw in Green Bay was a Best Buy store or something similar.

Lambeau Field is simply a special place to watch a professional football game. I can't imagine a more special venue. I have walked around and enjoyed the pre-game tailgating experience many times. One can't help but inhale the aroma of a nice bratwurst coming from a fan's portable barbecue. Entering the stadium bowl at Lambeau Field is a special event for a sports fan. It has that "wow" factor. My oldest son, Trevor, often teases me by saying that I am "with my people" when I go to Lambeau.

Perhaps one of the reasons I latched on to this team as a fan is because they are community owned, similar to the Winnipeg Blue Bombers. The community feel means a lot to me. I understand it. I should add that I have a permanent place at Lambeau Field. During my time working with the Winnipeg Football Club, a couple of my work colleagues surprised me one day. They presented me with a gift. It was a brick, one of those bricks you see at different sports venues these days. They're featured on a wall or walking path with your name on it and perhaps a message. My brick reads, "Jim Bell, Canada's No. 1 Fan," and there's a Packers' logo ("G") underneath. I must say I am proud of that brick and have made a point to visit it when I've had the opportunity to get back to Lambeau Field.

As the years passed, my connection with the Packers only grew stronger. The pinnacle of this connection came when I had the chance to witness them live at Lambeau Field in 1997. Helen and I were on vacation with the kids, enjoying a wonderful time in Wisconsin Dells. We made the drive to Green Bay, where I purchased two tickets to a game. This encounter, though just an exhibition game, left an indelible mark on me, mainly because I got to enjoy it with my son Trevor. Lambeau Field is, in my humble opinion, the holiest of grails for a football fan. I've been fortunate enough to make the pilgrimage there seven times. Attending a game at Lambeau Field isn't just a sports event; it's an experience like no other. All seven of these experiences carry memories that are etched into my heart.

My brick at Lambeau Field, home of the Green Bay Packers. So cool to have my name engraved there forever.

One trip that stands out took place in 2004. My two sons, Trev and Cory, my brother-in-law Henry, and his son Jordan embarked on an unforgettable adventure to see the Packers face the Dallas Cowboys. The journey began with a late-night drive from Winnipeg; we couldn't leave any earlier due to a touch football playoff game with our team, the Eagles. Driving through the night, Henry and I took turns at the wheel.

In the wee hours, in the heart of Minnesota, I saw flashing red lights in the rear-view mirror. Guilty of speeding, I braced for the inevitable. Just before the Minnesota state trooper approached, my son Trevor whispered, "Don't tell him we're going to Green Bay." Trevor was referring to the fact that Green Bay and Minnesota are archrivals on the football field. I was in enemy territory.

The officer did ask me where we were heading, and I responded with the truth. The officer chuckled. "Green Bay? You do know you're in Minnesota, right?" To our relief, he let us off with a warning and wished us well.

The game and the tailgating experience were exhilarating, but the true magic was in the camaraderie. Green Bay won the game, and that was the icing on the cake, but it was the shared moments with my family that made it extraordinary.

Another cherished memory was attending yet another Packers versus Cowboys game in the company of my son Trev, who happens to be a staunch Cowboys fan. It was an experience defined by laughter, rivalry, and football fandom.

In 2012, my daughter, Acksanna, and I made the trek to Green Bay to witness the Packers take on the Detroit Lions on a Sunday night. The day began with a hearty breakfast at IHOP, followed by a tour of Lambeau Field. People were tailgating from early morning, creating an electric atmosphere. We savoured every moment, making it an unforgettable father-daughter experience.

Then came the journey back to our hotel in Appleton. Post-game traffic in Green Bay is unlike anything else. It took us three hours to cover what's usually a thirty-minute drive. Hungry and exhausted, we settled for a late-night McDonald's run. Gobbling down a Big Mac, fries, and a chocolate shake at 2:00 a.m. does not make for a good night's sleep. It was an adventure we'll always treasure.

One more Green Bay Packers experience stands out, one I hadn't planned. In January 2008, when I was working for the Winnipeg Football Club, my boss, Lyle Bauer, surprised me with a ticket to the National Football Conference Championship Game in Green Bay. It was the Packers versus the New York Giants, with a trip to the Super Bowl on the line. The Packers lost in overtime, and I was there, alone. The stadium fell eerily silent as the Giants secured the win. It was a momentous game, but it lacked the shared excitement of previous trips. I was alone.

Football and the Packers have always been a part of my life, but these experiences have taught me an essential truth: Life, like football, is best enjoyed with those you love. Be it in a stadium packed with eighty thousand cheering fans or navigating the twists and turns of life, it's the people around you who make it all worthwhile. The game is fun to watch. Enjoying these experiences with people you love makes it priceless.

Eight

"A BAND OF BROTHERS"

How It Started

IN THE EARLY spring of 2002, my brother-in-law Jake decided to invite seven guys to his cabin at Brereton Lake to enjoy a couple of days of golf together. It turned out to be a really enjoyable and memorable time for all of us! During our last round on Sunday, it snowed and the course marshal had to kick us off.

I think it was meant to be a one-time outing with the boys, but the weekend was so much fun that we begged Jake to do it again the next year, and the year after that, and the year after that. We really didn't beg him; he knew he had to do it. I'm not sure if he initially intended this to be an annual event, but it has since evolved into a very special annual getaway, and every one of us looks forward to it. It's been a fixture on our calendars for twenty-two years and the tradition is still going strong.

So Many Memories

It isn't possible to capture the full twenty-three years of incredible memories we've shared. The best words I'd use to describe this group of men would be *unique*, *special*, *committed*, *competitive*, *trustworthy*, and *fiercely loyal*. It's a group of characters to be sure, but more importantly, they are men with an *abundance of character*.

What makes this group so special? Well, for one, it's the makeup. Some of us are family, while others are close friends. The age gap is wide, from twenty to sixty-five; I'm the old dude. We come from different walks of life in terms of our jobs and gifts.

This recipe has developed a special bond between us. Although we aren't all related to each other, we are a band of brothers. Sure, we enjoy golfing, and it's the magnet that draws us together once a year, but it's about so much more than the golf. It's truly about the relationships between us. There's that word again: "relationships."

To say that Jake's golf tournament has *evolved* into something special over the course of time would be an understatement. None of us take for granted Jake's commitment and generosity. He organizes the golf and ensures that we all have a comfortable place to sleep. He also feeds us like royalty! And he himself somehow still manages to play four solid rounds of golf!

How does he do it? He's a man of high character and integrity, strong as a horse, with a very caring, sensitive, generous, and selfless spirit. That's how he does it. It's his character, and he never grows tired of us. If he does, he certainly doesn't show it.

When the weekend starts, we always greet each other with big smiles and a lot of hugs. Some of us don't see each other often, so the hugs are heartfelt.

The weekend started with eight guys heading out to Jake's cabin at Brereton Lake on a Friday night, with two rounds on Saturday and one on Sunday. At the end, the winner was given a "green jacket" in a ceremony—a really ugly green jacket! Truth be told, I bought that jacket but have never earned the right to wear it. I can talk a big game, but I'm nowhere close to ever winning the jacket. Maybe this year … maybe next year …

Along the way, a new tradition formed. Those who were able to would take the Friday off would come out to Jake's cabin on Thursday night to get in a practice round on Friday and then head back and wait for the rest of our brothers to arrive safely on Friday evening. Well, as it turns out, for the past many years everyone makes it out on Thursday night, and the tourney is now four rounds of golf made up of two on Friday and one round on Saturday and Sunday. So special. And it's no longer eight guys but sixteen or eighteen, and Jake likely has a waiting list. One day soon, Jake will need to consider twenty guys or more! Maybe there will eventually be a qualifying round on Thursday. I wouldn't bet against it!

Who Are They?

Who are these guys who make up this band of brothers? Their names are Jake Kornelsen, Henry Kornelsen, Jeremy Kornelsen, Owen Kornelsen, Jordan Kornelsen, Curtis Duester, Paul Kornelsen, Sean Lehmann, Keenan Lehmann, Andy Regehr, Dave Neufeld, Rob Neufeld, Harry Neufeld, Miguel Texeira, Joel Stevens, Trevor Bell, Wilmar (Willy) Federau, Mark Warkentin, Tim Thiessen, Tim Toews, Nathan Gerhard, Karl Martens, and yours truly. And few others have also come for a weekend along the way.

"Our "Band of Brothers" at Granite Hills Golf Course, June 7, 2024. Such a special group! So many stories. It is my privilege to call them all my friends, my brothers.

One regular brother, Curt Wiebe, was part of the original group for years. He really loved to play. He was competitive, kind, principled, stubborn, and had a tremendous sense of humour. He also loved his Chicago Bears and would defend them even though they consistently stunk!

We lost Curt a few years ago to a dreaded ALS disease, but his memory and spirit live on. We miss him dearly.

I'll share one very memorable story. Unfortunately, Curt's illness was aggressive, and we all could see this very clearly. It was hard to watch. The last time he joined us on the golf weekend he couldn't actually play, but he did ride in a cart. During one round, he was in the group ahead of me on the golf course and he stepped out of the golf cart to hit a ball. He struggled mightily to hit the ball, and it travelled thirty yards at the most. I was surprised that he made contact with the ball. In typical Curt fashion, he threw his club in disgust. Well, we laughed from a distance as we watched him; however, we were also very close to tears. Curt was Curt right to his last day. The stories of Curt surface frequently. We miss you, buddy.

Here are a few more details about the golf weekend. We start on Friday morning, and in recent years have played at Granite Hills Golf Course. It's beautiful and certainly very challenging from a golf perspective. Over the years we've also played at Falcon Lake and Pinawa golf courses. They're also beautiful in their own way and put every golfer to the test. We split into foursomes and sometimes have five in a group, depending on the numbers. You share a cart with one other golfer and ride together for over four hours. I've had the privilege to ride with most of these men, my brothers. In my experience, we talk about everything, including family, work, sports, spirituality, the challenges of life—I think you get the picture. There's never a shortage of things to talk about. We laugh, we lean on each other, and we also add a little bit of trash talk in good fun. And we offer up some encouragement too. Maybe I didn't realize it in the early years, but the conversations bind us together. There's a deep sense of trust. Nothing is off the table when we're chatting.

On Friday afternoon (the second round), you're with three different guys. Of course, I will then ride with somebody different in the cart. More dialogue, more relationships built, more trust, just more everything. Personally, I find this so inspiring. They may not know it, but their kinship means everything to me.

Whether we want to admit it or not, come Friday night we're already dogged tired, at least I am. We break bread together and share in more conversation, including a lot of sports trivia, which seems to be an annual ritual. And we eat some more when Jake hauls out the wings later in the evening. The guys all bring drinks, baking, and treats to share. We go to bed tired and full, resting up for round number three on Saturday morning.

We're up very early on Saturday morning, back at it again. We share breakfast together, and my guess is we all think we're going to shoot the lights out this round. After all, it's "moving day," as they say on television on the PGA. Once again, ride with someone different in the cart and enjoy the round with two other guys. This just never gets old, not for any of us.

Amongst all the fun and laughter, I have to say I learn from these guys, even as the elder statesman. You're never too old to learn from someone.

I think it's fair to say that we all have baggage in life. Spending a weekend together over golf, good food, and fellowship allows us to park the baggage for a few days. Often we open up and talk about the baggage, the challenges of life. I want to repeat that there is a foundation of loyalty and trust within this group that makes it easier to have some deep conversations.

On a lighter note, I've mentioned a few times that we share a cart with different guys in each of the first three rounds. I enjoy this part immensely, but I wonder sometimes about how the guys feel about being stuck with me for four to five hours. I am not quiet. I'll often start a conversation. It's fun to chat with my riding partner and the other two guys in the foursome, and I like to poke a little fun at everyone—maybe more than a little. The fact is, I think I'd get tired of myself if I had to ride with me for a round of golf. Does that make sense? I don't know if it's my gift or a curse. Ask one of the fellas! But if I can help the guys laugh, I am more than willing to do it. Also, I like to listen to them. Hopefully they find this helpful. I do. I sure appreciate their company and the camaraderie. Thank you, my brothers—you mean the world to me. Do you have a group of people like this in your life? If you do, treasure it. What a blessing.

Then comes Saturday night, with more good food, more conversation and sports trivia, and the annual "Texas Hold 'Em" card game. Everyone's eyes start to get a little heavy as the evening moves along. Three rounds of golf over two days will do that to us, especially as we get older.

We wake up on Sunday morning and prepare for the last round, and this time we're grouped based on order of finish through the first three rounds. The best four tee-off last as they battle it out for weekend golf supremacy and the coveted green jacket. The tradition is that the rest of us form the gallery around the eighteenth green as the final group makes their way to putt on the final hole. There is cheering and heckling and then the handshakes. Then it's back to the cabin or Jake's home for a BBQ. We pack up and head home with more treasured memories. Every one of these annual weekends has been such an awesome experience, I wish I could write more about it, as I could easily fill pages and pages.

Makes Me Pause and Think

As I write this, a thought and question come to my mind: *Is life similar in some ways to a golf game?* Think about it.

We all have a beginning in life, call it our "tee time." In golf, we start on the first hole and play eighteen holes. Life is similar, figuratively speaking, so work with me as you read further. Some play a shorter course, and life on earth ends sooner than for others. Again, I think of Curt. He played a shorter course in life, and I believe he played it well.

As I think about it, at age sixty-four I know I'm playing the "back nine" of life. I hope I have six or seven holes left as I do the math. I need to be thankful for every hole I can play. Nobody is going to par the course in life. Every now and then we can rejoice with a par, birdie, or eagle, but we're all going to bogey our share. But by the grace of God, we often get a chance to respond, hit it again. Can you relate to this? You don't have to be a golfer to understand.

As I golf with my brothers, parts of some courses are absolutely beautiful and you simply want to take it all in. For me personally, I think of the second hole at Falcon Lake very early on a Friday or Saturday morning in July. At times I've stood in the middle of that fairway looking at the trees, and sometimes even wildlife runs by, like a deer, fox, coyote, or even a bear. You can also hear the road noise coming from the highway and see the cars driving by. It's just one of those special moments when I stop, look heavenward, and whisper a prayer and thank God for the splendour of His creation and for the people I get to enjoy this with.

We can certainly all agree that life has its challenges to say the least. I hope it's good advice when I say that sometimes we just need to stop and be still. Do you have those times when things slow down enough for you to be still and count your blessings? The psalmist says it best in Psalm 46:10a: *"Be still, and know that I am God ..."* It's a simple and short verse with a lot of merit. In life and on the course, take time to be still; it's good for the soul. Smell the roses and give thanks to God above for everything, including those with whom we get to experience life.

In the game of golf there are bunkers, water hazards, and the "rough," and all these elements make the game more challenging. We try to stay away from these hazards, but we're simply not perfect golfers. And we're not perfect as human beings. Sorry to break it to you! Sometimes we make the same mistake two or three times in a row, like me in a sand trap. Let me tell you, it's not pretty to watch. Once again, I compare this to life—my life, anyway.

If I'm honest, every decision I make I try to stay in the "fairway of life," as it makes things so much easier. I certainly don't look forward to my next shot, my next decision after I make a mistake. Like in golf, I am far from perfect in life. Ask those I golf with and those I do life with! I wonder sometimes if those difficult spots I find myself in aren't there for me to try and build some character. I don't play golf to perfection, and I often fall short in life as well. We are not perfect golfers, and we are not perfect in life. In golf, my buddies will sometimes give me a replay, a "mulligan," to hit the shot again. In life, I thank God for second chances. I think that's called God's grace. Can you relate to any of this? Perhaps golf isn't your thing, but I think you get my point.

On the golf course, we laugh at each other, and sometimes we just encourage each other. Should life be any different? There are some days when the bunkers and hazards of life appear, and they can be unexpected and even exhausting. We need that encouragement to help us get through. Some things in life are simply long par fives that call on us to persevere and endure, but we don't have to do it alone. During some very difficult times I've turned to God for His comforting hand and guidance, and I've felt most content in the storm. I also lean on the love and support of those who are precious to me. So don't do it alone in life. Lean on Him and those close to you, God's grace and loving people. God hands out mulligans too; we just need to ask Him. He grants us forgiveness through His grace. As we receive it, we also need to extend it to others. He commands us to do so.

After nine holes on the course, it's a chance to take a break, grab a coffee or snack, and recharge. Maybe we need to do that more as well during life. Take a break, have a coffee with a friend or loved one, and get ready for the next challenge. In golf, we have to get ready to play the next hole, and life is really no different, with more activities and decisions to be made. So often I say after eighteen holes, "If I had done this ... made a different decision ... been a little less careless." I don't know when I'll play the eighteenth hole in life, but that tee box and fairway are much closer than they used to be. If I took the opportunity to look back over the eighteen holes of life, what would I say? What do I want said? Would I play life's course any differently? If the answer is yes, then I should simply do it now. It's like reaching into your golf bag and using a different club. As I often say to the guys, "Don't leave anything in the bag." I don't know what it means, but it sounds good and leaves the guys scratching their heads and chuckling a bit.

How Do I Translate All This?

So what have I come to know, or think I know?

Life is a gift; golf is a game. I am fortunate to have experienced life thus far with many beautiful people, including my family (my wife and my kids, their families, and my extended family), and with some very special friends. I've been truly blessed to meet a lot of people along the way. They've made a real difference in my life.

I play golf with some amazing friends, special men—my brothers.

Golf isn't fun when you play alone; it wouldn't be the same without these guys. I don't think life is meant to be done alone. I've been so blessed in this regard. I hope that there are some playoff holes that extend this one day, but if not, I am surely grateful.

The green jacket is the prize that goes to our weekend champion on the Sunday, the best golfer at Jake's tournament. It's quite an accomplishment. The pros on television play for their prized green jacket once a year at the Master's Tournament. This made me think too.

In the end, who is my Master? When the course of life is done and I'm walking off the eighteenth hole, I'll look forward to meeting my Master. I don't know exactly what that will look like, but I imagine I'll have a chance to speak, to give account. If I'm right, I hope I get a chance to say thank you to my Master and to acknowledge these men. I will thank God and say how fortunate and blessed I was to have shared life with them on and off the course. They mean that much to me.

In summary, this annual golf event is special for all the reasons I spoke about and the experiences we've all shared. For you the reader, whether it's golf or something else, I hope you have a circle of friends like this group. May it be that you have deep and trusting relationships around you as you play the "course of life." Again, I am certain that life is not meant to be done alone.

Note: At Jake's tournament in June 2022, I asked the guys to write a few things down and share what this annual tournament means to them. They know that I'm writing a personal memoir and am including a piece about our friendships and specifically this golf tournament. Below are some examples of what they shared so freely:

> "This time together recharges me. It helps me see that there are still good men around, and I am humbled to be able to participate. (He used the following words to describe the group and weekend: brotherhood, community, grace, acceptance, love, forgiveness, blessings, and joy)."

> "For twenty years, I have been coming to this weekend to enjoy the company of these men and the activities we love. If it's true that a person can be judged by the average of the people around him, I have to apologize for bringing down the average. I enjoy the golf, the meals, the lake, but the real value of this time and group is the knowledge that I have a group of people who are in my life that support me, are there for me, and are family in every sense of the word. I am in the very fortunate position to share this weekend with my son. There are no better examples of how to live a life, be a man of integrity, how to support each other, than the gathering of this group. Not lost in this is the spectacular example of generosity, love, and support that Jake has on display to this group of men. This is an important and best part of my life, and I am beyond grateful to be included."

> "This is a weekend away for rejuvenation and revitalization. It means a time spent with God-loving men. It means time spent with friends and family that I wouldn't necessarily see too often. It means having wonderful conversations in a vehicle for two and a half hours. It means asking personal questions to your paired partner in the

golf cart. It means laughter and games. It means looking up to men I love and admire and seeing what it means to be a friend. And it means being inspired to be *that* kind of man for my children, nephews, and friends."

"I am so amazed what a wonderful group of guys these are to hang out with. I was very nervous about not fitting in when I came for the first time about twelve years ago. May God richly bless all the guys here, starting from Jake and Henry on down to the young ones."

"A long time ago, life was very hectic for me. So I decided to take a bunch of guys away for a weekend, and golf was something in common with the guys I hung around with. I soon found out we all had problems we were dealing with, and this weekend was a way to leave all of that behind. And now this weekend means so much to all of us and it has grown to bringing in young men and mentoring them into awesome men that will make a difference in the lives of others. I can see it already in their lives and I am so proud of all the men that come out. I love them all. May we keep this alive as long as we live. Great friendships have been born here."

Beyond the Golf Weekend

I should add that there is more to these friendships than just the golf tournament once a year. Some of the guys see each other quite frequently during the year, including breakfast every Friday morning at 7:00 a.m. for those who can make it. I'm not a regular attendee, but I enjoy it when I can make it. More conversation, more laughter, and sometimes serious dialogue.

During the winter, Jake has started another tradition whereby he will invite us all to the cabin for a weekend during the NFL playoffs. This is another tremendous time of getting together. We're all football fans and have our favourite teams that we cheer for, but the weekend is much more than just about watching football. We'll arrive Friday night and sit around to catch up, play cards and sports trivia, etc. Get up and go for breakfast at a fine little restaurant close to Jake's cabin and then back to play "shinny" on the lake. This is when we all pretend to be a lot younger and we end up humbling ourselves. Just have a look at us when we're done! Nobody is moving too fast. Yet another weekend of fun and bonding.

As I reflect on these precious experiences with my buddies, I think it's fair to say that it's a testament to the power of long-lasting friendships. The tradition of this weekend getaway and the togetherness of this band of brothers has allowed us to create many cherished memories. At the heart of this is the importance of character and support in life's journey. I encourage everyone to value your own relationships and appreciate the beauty and challenges of life together.

Nine

MY WORK EXPERIENCES—
FROM PAPER ROUTES TO THE CFL

I HAVE BEEN very fortunate in my work career. My education and university degree prepared me well. I believe that the experiences I accumulated along the way also warranted me the opportunity to test my leadership skills. I won't write about the all the jobs I held, but I will highlight a few very special ones and share what comes to my mind.

Learning Responsibility

My first job was a paper route. I was just a youngster, about the age of eleven or twelve. I was lucky enough to deliver papers on my side of the street where I lived—you guessed it, Dominion Street.

Earlier on I mentioned a friend by the name of Al. He was one of our regulars in the schoolyard. Al was an athletic kid who lived on the same street as me, just further down the block. We shared the paper route and the money. Sure, it was work, but it was also fun, especially at Christmas. The tips were so good! The paper route was my first opportunity to learn about commitment and responsibility. To this day when I drive down Dominion Street, I can remember many of the houses I delivered to. It's another treasured experience. I can remember the thrill associated with getting a "start." A start meant that someone new on the delivery route wanted to receive a newspaper every day. The more papers you delivered, the more money you made. It's the equivalent of getting a raise. Getting a "stop" was not good news, for obvious reasons. Maybe this was another life lesson about learning to take the good with the bad. What do we call that as adults? Rolling with the punches?

I got my first full-time summer job in 1975, before I turned sixteen. My mom worked at Old Dutch Foods and asked the boss if they might have room for a young freckle-faced kid. I got the job stacking boxes of chips in the factory and doing other stuff, including loading semi-trailers. The part I enjoyed the most was loading the semis as the boxes of chips would come out of the plant on a conveyor belt. There would be two guys on either side of the conveyor belt throwing boxes to two others. The guys catching the boxes would have to catch them and stack them quickly and efficiently. Sometimes one of these large boxes would hit you in the face or in another sensitive area, and a fight would break out. Fights didn't happen often, but from time to time there would be a short slugfest. Boys will be boys!

I learned a lot on that job, including what it's like to have to get up very early in the morning. My shift started at 7:00 a.m. I found it difficult to rise that early five days a week. Another lesson learned: discipline yourself to be on time. By the way, my starting wage was $2.37/hour, and I thought I had won the lottery. I needed the money, as I'd already made up my mind to attend university in a few years. I would work at Old Dutch Foods during the summers of 1975 and 1976, when I was fifteen and sixteen years old. I was very grateful for that job. Thank you, Mom, for talking to your boss at the time and getting me much-needed employment.

I can remember reading a brochure one day that I found in our mailbox while I was in grade 12. The Canada Revenue Agency (CRA) was hiring for seasonal term positions. Those interested in applying would have to take a math aptitude test. That's right, math, right in my wheelhouse! I took the test and did very well. As a result, I got one of the better paying positions for that spring and summer. In the spring, I worked in the evenings and then full-time during the day in the summer. The pay was very good and the work fit my skill set very well.

Settling into a Career

I graduated in 1981 from the University of Manitoba, and my first job was with the CRA as an auditor. My work experience was very helpful in landing this job. I stayed with CRA until 1985 and moved on to work in public practice, and then a few stops in property management, a non-profit organization, and even went on my own for a few years doing income tax returns and preparing financial statements for small businesses. After a short time at Palliser Furniture, the phone rang in March 2002. I was not expecting what happened next.

The Phone Call That Changed Everything

This call would be a life-changer for me. *Truly it would be*. Let me set the stage for this telephone conversation. The call came from a person at a local personnel agency, someone I'd never met or spoken to previously. I was sitting in my office at Palliser Furniture. It was a good job, and I could even walk to work, which was an added bonus.

The personnel agent explained that she'd gotten my name and resume from someone and that there was a job opportunity available I might be interested in. She wouldn't disclose the name of the organization over the phone, but she invited me to her office to discuss the position. I almost turned her down immediately. I explained that I wasn't looking to make a change, but as it turned out, I was going to be close to her office in the next few days. I told her that I didn't want to waste her time. Anyway, I committed to go and meet with her. Wise decision—lucky, but wise!

Later that week, we met and she started to explain that there was a very well-known organization in Winnipeg looking for a director of finance. I didn't flinch—not yet. Then came the moment. She mentioned that the "CEO, Lyle Bauer" had hired their firm to conduct the search. That's when I interrupted.

"Lyle Bauer, CEO of the Winnipeg Blue Bombers?"

She confirmed my thought and told me that she knew I'd be interested. I believe my next words were something to the effect of asking her to forget all that I had said to this point, and that I was indeed very interested. What an understatement! We went on to have a wonderful interview.

About a week or so later, I went to the offices of the Winnipeg Football Club. I was about to be interviewed by Lyle Bauer in his office. I was so excited and nervous to meet him. I impatiently waited in the reception area.

What an opportunity! In short, I remember thinking that our first meeting went extremely well. We talked about the Bombers of course, and the requirements of the job. We also talked a lot about our families. I'm confident in saying that Lyle saw that I had a passion for the Bombers and that he'd get a strong commitment from me in performing the requirements of the job.

Frankly, I didn't think that I got the job, as it took some time to hear back from the personnel agent. However, I was advised to remain patient (Patient? Really?) as she explained to me that Lyle was a very busy man and it may take a few weeks for him to make a decision. I really wanted this job, a dream job, so patience was not in abundance.

I had a second interview, which also went well. Soon after that, Lyle called me back and I was hired as the director of finance of the Winnipeg Football Club. I will remember that day forever. It really changed my life. Lyle was in the midst of having to attend several meetings out of town in the coming days. He apologized for making me the offer over the phone. Wow, there was no need to apologize, as I was absolutely thrilled. It took five minutes or less for us to finalize the details. My first day as director of finance with the Winnipeg Football Club was April 7, 2002. This was so very special, as I was going to get paid to go to work for an organization I had followed and supported for as long as I could remember.

Initiated!

Here's a funny story from when I began my journey with the Big Blue. Lyle had an initiation tradition for new employees of the Winnipeg Football Club, and there was no avoiding it. It wasn't so much an initiation as a welcome to the organization. At a staff meeting in the boardroom, "rookie" employees were required to stand and sing a song of their choice for all employees to hear and then of course laugh at you. I chose to sing a version of Neil Diamond's "Song Sung Blue." However, I composed different lyrics and called it "Bomber Blue." I certainly made a fool of myself, but I remember all the staff joining me in singing the chorus to my own words, and it was a blast. Lyle had tears in his eyes from laughing so hard. I was now officially part of the office team, and it felt so good.

My first few years in my role of Director of Finance were good. I looked forward to going to work every day, and that's no stretch of the imagination. There was so much to learn within this dynamic organization. This organization has always been a gem as seen through the eyes of our city and province. At the outset, I said it was a privilege to be hired there. I was so

PATHS OF FAITH, BONDS OF LOVE

fortunate, and I don't think I ever took this opportunity for granted. I was motivated like never before in my career path.

I must say that I was also very humbled. Let me explain. Perhaps you're a bit like me in that you consider yourself to be a fan of the game of football. If not, please keep reading anyway. Before commencing my employment with the Blue Bomber organization, I considered myself to be a very knowledgeable football fan. You know, I thought I knew everything. I can watch a game and "second guess" with the best of them.

Well, wrong! It didn't take me long to determine that I knew very little. There is so much to learn within the front office of a sports organization with many moving parts. Please allow me to let you down gently if you think you know all the "ins" and "outs" of the game. There is so much more to the game than meets the eye. Whether we're in the stands or watching with friends in front of the television, we only see the final product. We see the big run, spectacular catches, and bone-crushing hits. We are entertained. I got more than a glimpse of the preparation that takes place before a game. I had a front row seat for all of this, and it humbled me to realize how little I knew. Oh, and then there's the business side of the game, including salary cap management. Don't forget about coaches and players being fired and released. They are human and have families too. I hope this abbreviated summary of my experiences early on with the organization paints a clear picture for you.

The first few years were incredible in so many ways. I marveled at the complexities and dynamics of the professional football world. Little did I know that these early years weren't just about learning the ropes but about laying the groundwork for a potential pivotal moment. It all began with a phone call. I remember that call as though it happened yesterday. Another memorable phone call would take place a few years in, a call you never want to receive.

Another Phone Call

After a few short years with the club, I was made aware of some very tough news. It was on a Sunday, soon after we got home from church. Helen and I were having lunch and the phone rang. It was my boss, Lyle Bauer. He apologized for interrupting my Sunday and asked me to come to the office to meet with him at 2:00 p.m. that day. I said certainly, and my heart was racing when I got off the phone. This was indeed rare, as Lyle had never called me on the weekend. Maybe an occasional email or text, but not a phone call.

I remember calling my late dear friend Jerry Maslowsky, our VP of sales and marketing at the time. I asked if he knew anything, and he said no. But he'd also been asked to come in that day, at 2:30, so thirty minutes after me. My mind was playing through all the scenarios as I drove to the office. Were we making a player trade and Lyle needed some info on player salaries? Was there something new to report on a potential new stadium? I was wrong on these assumptions and whatever else came to my mind. What was going on, and why the phone call?

I arrived at the office and went directly to Lyle's office. The news that Lyle delivered was shocking and had nothing to do with football. It was much more important than football. It was about life.

Lyle sat me down and explained that he'd been diagnosed with an aggressive form of throat cancer. He told me he was going to fight it as best he could. I must say that if I've met any man in my life who was not afraid of a fight, it was Lyle. He had the mentality of an offensive lineman. He had learned throughout his football career how to scratch and claw for every inch of turf. After telling me about his cancer, he told me that he wanted the club to operate smoothly in his absence. He was going to be away for an extended period while recovering. He wanted me to take on a leadership role during his absence. The chair of the board joined us in the meeting that afternoon, and I remember him asking me if I was up to the task. My response was, "I will do anything for Lyle and the club." I didn't really know if I was ready—likely not. However, I was motivated to keep the Blue Bomber ship sailing as best I could and rely on some key people around me. I did my very best in Lyle's absence. He had entrusted me to lead, so I owed it to him, the organization, and our fans to commit myself to my best effort.

It was certainly an emotional time. Sure, Lyle was known as a former championship football player and sharp executive. I also know he was a devoted family man to his wife, Heidi, and three children. We shared this in common, and seeing him around his family only deepened my respect for him. This was likely the main reason for my response to the challenge at hand, and why I would do anything for Lyle and the organization.

I Continue to Grow at the Winnipeg Football Club

Lyle did recover and returned to the office after his period of recovery. We were all glad to see him again. He fought so hard to recover. I learned so much while Lyle was away. I was motivated and inspired to lead to the best of my ability. One of the things I learned was that I was not ready to be the CEO of the Winnipeg Football Club. Not yet.

However, that time also taught me about trying to be a leader and about building trust with people around you. A very valuable lesson indeed. One of the initial challenges was to "earn" the respect of the office team. Sure, they knew me by now, but Lyle left big leadership shoes to fill. I wasn't about to make radical changes. Keep the ship sailing in the right direction and encourage everyone to work as a team off the field. This may have been the time that I learned about my leadership philosophy and style. I believe in collaborative leadership. Learn to listen to those around you; they have good ideas to share and implement. Servant leadership is high on my list. This time allowed me to put these into practice. I also believe these leadership principles formed the foundation of who I tried to be as a leader in the workplace. I know I made mistakes, but I don't think I ever wavered from that foundation.

Promoted

I remained in my role as director of finance until the end of the 2005 year. In 2006, the Winnipeg Football Club was awarded the privilege of hosting the Grey Cup game. This had only been done twice before in Winnipeg's history, in 1991 and 1998. The entire organization and our community of passionate football fans were very excited. I was about to find out that it was a tremendous amount of work to organize an event of this magnitude. I had never been involved in planning such a large event like this before.

I was promoted to vice president of finance at the beginning of 2006. I was assigned a significant amount of responsibility in preparation for the Grey Cup. I embraced it, and I enjoyed every bit of it. What an experience!

We dressed up our old stadium as best we could. It was over fifty years old at the time. I believe the stadium was shining for the whole country to see on that late afternoon and evening in November 2006. The Winnipeg

Football Club hosted a very successful Grey Cup, in my opinion. The game was sold out, with close to fifty thousand fans on hand to watch it live. The B.C. Lions were victorious over the Montreal Alouettes. As exciting as it was to plan and host the Grey Cup, it's not something you want to do every year. It's a mountain of work! I learned so much through this unique experience. It took the combined efforts of all of our staff, government officers, community sponsors, and on and on. It was the most rewarding teamwork exercise I had ever been part of, and I remain most grateful for it.

Significant Changes

The team made it to the Grey Cup Game in 2007, but we lost to the Saskatchewan Roughriders. We lost our starting quarterback the week before due to injury, so that didn't help matters.

The team made the playoffs in 2008 and lost the first playoff game. A decision was made to fire the head coach, which was surprising to many. One thing about the business of professional football is that change happens, and it can happen quickly.

I need to fast forward to the 2009 season. The Winnipeg Football Club experienced a very challenging season both on and off the field. Our CEO and the man who'd hired me, Lyle Bauer, resigned in December 2009. I was asked by the board of directors to assume the responsibilities as interim president of the WFC. This would be an absolute honour and privilege. I was humbled to the core. I accepted this role, and in February 2010, the "interim" tag was removed. I was now the president of the Winnipeg Football Club. What a dream, and again, what an honour! I can't help but think back to those schoolyard days. And now here I am as president of the Blue Bombers. Writing this still brings a smile to my face, and even some disbelief.

Along with me, we also had new leadership in the football operations area of the club. Joe Mack was announced as the new general manager, and Paul LaPolice was named the new head coach. I remember attending numerous public events in 2010 and 2011 as president of the club, and I did a lot of public speaking. I really enjoyed this part of the role. I did my very best as president to represent the organization and be an ambassador for the Blue Bombers.

The most rewarding experience for me was having the opportunity to meet the fans, not just locally but across the province of Manitoba. There are truly no fans like Blue Bomber fans. I learned to appreciate each and every one of them. Blue Bomber fans are passionate, loyal, and encouraging. I grew to love the fan base.

I Can't Do This on My Own

I remember vividly game one of the regular season in 2010. It was my first game as president. I asked my wife to come to the office early that day, in the afternoon. Game time was likely 7:30 p.m. I was so nervous, pacing through the office all day. By the way, Helen was not much of a football fan until I joined the Bomber organization. However, after that—wow! What did I create? Helen picked up "Blue Bomber fever" and became as passionate as all of our fans. On that particular day, I had arranged with our equipment manager to allow me to take an old practise football. I didn't tell him why.

Helen met me at the office, and we drove to "Garbage Hill" in the west end, about five minutes from Canad Inns Stadium. I got out of the car and proceeded to write a note on the football with a sharpie marker. I wrote a prayer on the football, and I addressed it to God. Why? I knew that I needed God's guiding hand and provisions to lead the Bomber organization. I also knew I couldn't do it on my own merit. I believe God placed me in this position not because I was the most qualified but maybe for "such a time as this." I said a prayer with Helen standing right beside me and threw the ball to the heavens. I threw it as high as I could throw it. I don't know where that ball landed. Maybe God caught the ball! You know, a completed pass. I believe in my heart of hearts to this day that God answered that prayer. I will never forget that day.

More Memories

There are just way too many fond memories to share of the Blue Bomber experience, so I'll limit myself to sharing just a few, or try to, anyway. I may repeat myself here, but I want to go back a few steps. As I mentioned earlier, as an organization we experienced a very difficult and tumultuous year in 2009, both on and off the field. There were circumstances that led to our game attendance decreasing significantly after the Banjo Bowl in September 2009.

The Banjo Bowl is the annual home game held in September. It's virtually a guaranteed sellout crowd. The week previous, on the Labour Day weekend, the Blue Bombers make the trek to Regina to play the Roughriders. They come to our house the following week. It's a very intense rivalry, and respectful for the most part. In my opinion, it's the best rivalry in the Canadian Football League. The stadiums are normally filled to capacity on both weekends, and the fans really get into it, to say the least.

In 2009, the Riders came to Winnipeg and laid a severe beating on us. I know they put up over fifty points on us that day. The game couldn't end quick enough. We were embarrassed, and our fans let us know it. It's one thing to lose games but quite another to be severely humbled by your archrival in your own back yard. That loss, coupled with some challenging internal events within the organization, led to a very trying and challenging finish to the season, both on and off the field.

Attendance dropped by six or seven thousand seats a game for the last remaining home games after the Riders beat us. Remember, at that time I was the vice president of finance. Add up the negative financial impact of significant losses in attendance, concession sales, and retail sales and it's not a pretty picture. And it's not a fun financial picture to present to your boss and to the board of directors.

We were bleeding money, and the integrity of the organization was suffering as well, in my opinion. I sensed that changes had to take place at the end of the season. I didn't know the magnitude of what they would be. Personnel changes would likely have to happen on the field and in football operations. I also wondered if changes might happen in the front office, given all that took place that year. We didn't make the playoffs. But what would happen? What changes were going to be made? I certainly didn't know, as these decisions would be made by those above me in the organization.

I was certainly feeling anxious, and our staff at the time was on pins and needles because they cared about the club. Working for the Bombers was more than just a job to these people.

Yet Another Phone Call

The answer would become known the week before Christmas. Our oldest son, Trevor, was getting married in Brandon on December 18, 2009. Helen and I made our way to Brandon the day before to help decorate the church and with other preparations. I was with Trev the day before the wedding when my cell phone rang a couple of times. The first call came from my boss, Lyle Bauer.

Before writing about that phone call, I need to say that I had developed a tremendous amount of respect for Lyle over the years. He played the game as an offensive lineman and he's a Grey Cup champion. His competitive nature stayed with him as president and CEO of the Bombers. I've seen it many times. I remember one time in particular when I was sitting in his office. Lyle knew that I had a real passion for the game, so anytime we could talk football, I certainly appreciated his time and willingness to engage in such conversation. During this particular chat, Lyle got going on the "pureness" of the game. He got up out of his chair and pointed to the battlefield of play outside of his office window. He passionately and clearly pointed out to me that the game is pure. "It is you against him; it is us against them. It's mano versus mano. There is no ___ out there (He used strong language!)."

I remember his eyes getting as big as saucers as he made his way around his desk and pointed at me and told me to always remember that. I think I recall this experience because I thought he was going to use me as a tackling dummy. I was scared he was going to hit me (not really, of course). He was going to show me how to lay out a guy that stood between him and the goal line. Lucky me! Before Lyle battled cancer, he was all of six-feet-four-inches tall and a very big, strong man. There was a presence about him.

Lyle knew the game on the field and he knew the football business. He trained me and allowed me every opportunity to learn about the organization from pillar to post. I will always appreciate Lyle for hiring me, teaching me, and preparing me for leadership opportunities. Thank you, Lyle.

Back to the phone call on December 17, 2009. Lyle informed me that he had let the board of directors know that he was resigning. I sense there had been some very difficult discussions between Lyle and the board. He also told me that I would likely hear from the board chair soon. The board would ask me to take on the role of interim president. I was silent as Lyle spoke. I had no idea what to say, as I was filled with so many feelings and emotions. On one hand, I had so much respect for Lyle, and I knew this had to be a very hard decision for him. For those who got to know Lyle, he certainly had that tough and gruff outer layer, and he was quite a physical presence. Underneath all that was a man with a very caring heart who was fiercely loyal.

I was also numb by the thought that I'd become the next president of the WFC. Lyle said some real nice things that day on the phone, and he told me that I was ready, that I had earned the opportunity to lead the Winnipeg Football Club. That meant the world to me coming from Lyle. As a quick side note, I can remember him addressing me a the "Bomber CEO Wannabe" on several occasions. He would challenge me with an issue and ask me "So, CEO Wannabe, how would you solve this?" I may not have seen it then, but perhaps Lyle was grooming me.

I was deeply saddened recently to find out that Lyle passed away in the spring of 2024. I attended his Celebration of Life on August 22, 2024—his birthday. There was laughter and tears as stories were shared. It was wonderful to reconnect with so many familiar faces from my time with the Blue Bomber organization. It was like a family reunion. Lyle touched the lives of many people, including me. I will always be so grateful to Lyle for hiring me.

Shortly after Lyle's call, the phone rang again. It was our board chair, the late Ken Hildahl, a wonderful man. Ken officially asked me to take the reigns of the club as interim president. I was so honoured, I said yes immediately. I got off the phone, and the first person I told was my son Trevor, as he was close beside me. Trev was so proud and happy for me, as were Helen, Cory, and Acksanna. I know I was very emotional after receiving the call from Mr. Hildahl. And all of this was happening while preparing for our son's wedding the next day. What timing! But then again, God's timing is always perfect.

I was new to the president's chair, and at the same time the board hired a new general manager of football operations and a head coach. This was significant change to say the least. I didn't know our new general manager, Joe Mack, at all. I knew Coach Paul Lapolice, but not well, as he'd been an assistant coach with the team a few years prior under head coach Dave Ritchie. We had our first press conference the week following the announcement of the changes. This was the beginning of a relationship between the three of us for the next few years.

I knew I had my work cut out for me immediately, given what had transpired in the 2009 season. I believe the first thing I did after my media interviews was meet with my executive team and then our entire staff. My message was this: The bad news is that our integrity as an organization has been damaged, and our passionate fan base has lost some confidence in the organization. The good news, and I truly believed this, was that we could restore the integrity of the WFC in the fan's eyes. However, it was going to take a lot of work and commitment from all of us. This would be a test as to how well we could work together as a front office team. We would have to earn back their trust. We couldn't be inner focused; we had to go to them. It was about restoring and building trust and critical relationships.

Earlier I wrote about our committed and devoted staff. This was an example of that, as everyone was committed. Our staff would grow close, as we cared for one another. Yes, we wanted to earn the trust and favour of the fan base, and through all of what was to come, our group became tight. I don't like to misuse the word "family," but if there is such a thing as a staff morphing into a family, this was it. I can remember on so many occasions having conversations with people in my office that had nothing to do with football. We often talked and helped each other with life challenges. We listened to each other. I grew to love these people.

Taking the Show on the Road

We developed an aggressive marketing plan whereby we would take the "Bomber Message" to as many communities as possible. I felt it was very important to connect with our fans as best we could. Let's let them know we appreciated their dedication, loyalty, and passion for the Blue Bombers. We'd also let them know that we were going to work very hard to restore their confidence in the team and the organization.

It seemed like we went everywhere, and I had so many speaking engagements. I enjoyed every one of them. One of the most rewarding parts of the job was meeting with countless passionate Bomber fans and corporate sponsors. To this day I cherish the memories of meeting so many wonderful people. Through all of this, I believe I learned something about myself. I enjoy meeting people and getting to know them, whether they're football fans or from all walks of life. This energizes me. In my opinion, you can't beat meeting and connecting with people. This was such a rewarding part of the job as president of the Winnipeg Football Club.

One experience sticks out—well, maybe more than one. The vice president of sales and marketing at the time, Jerry Maslowsky, and I were invited to the Brandon Chamber of Commerce to have lunch and meet the mayor of Brandon. This took place early in 2010, so I was still quite green as the president of the WFC. They fed us like kings with chicken, ribs, and all the extras.

When the lunch was over, we began our discussion about the Bombers, and I recall the mayor looking straight into my eyes and asking, "Where have you guys been? Those of you who work for the Bombers have 'perimeteritis.' You never leave the city. We have Bomber fans out here too, you know. And a lot of people in Brandon now cheer for the Saskatchewan Roughriders." Ouch, that one really hurt.

I sat there and listened and listened some more. It was difficult to hear and absorb this, but very important for me to listen. I think at one point I tried to interject with something I wanted to say, but the mayor told me he wasn't done. So I listened some more, again a valuable life exercise as I recall. When the mayor was done, he invited me to respond.

I told him he was right, that the club hadn't done a good job at reaching out to the wonderful community of Brandon. I asked him to give us a chance to earn back their trust and support. Jerry and I knew we had a big job in front of us, and this was only one community. Granted, Brandon is a big community! I should add that the team held one day of training camp in Brandon in 2010. This was well received by the community.

Building Blocks

The 2010 season was also challenging but in a different way. Whereas in 2009 the team on the field struggled mightily and was in decline, I could see that the 2010 team was much different in a positive way. We didn't make the playoffs, but the team was improving week after week. We lost so many close games, but the fans stayed with us.

I commented earlier that Blue Bomber fans are extremely loyal and supportive. This was an example of those traits. They could see that we were on the right track. This was definitely a year of transition with three new leaders running the organization and many changes on the field.

Brandon wasn't the only place we went, as it seemed we travelled throughout the whole province to engage with Bomber fans and the business community everywhere. As I recall, we went to Portage la Prairie, Winkler, Morden, and many more towns and places. I remember we were also invited out to Kenora, Ontario to participate in their Chamber of Commerce dinner. Every place we went we were welcomed with open arms. It was fun and very encouraging. This would pay dividends down the road.

A Game Ball

One precious memory from the 2010 season comes from the home game against the B.C. Lions or Thanksgiving Monday. We'd been struggling to win games, but we were getting better. We were losing this game well into the fourth quarter, and fans were leaving early, but the team simply refused to quit. We came back to tie the game and it went into overtime. We won the game when one of our defensive players intercepted a pass and returned it for a touchdown. The fans went crazy; it was so loud and exciting. As the team was celebrating on the field, Coach LaPolice invited me into the locker room. During his post-game celebratory speech, he awarded me the game ball in front of the team. How special was that! I remember speaking and thanking the team for their tremendous effort that day; they were awesome. I have that game ball to this day. It was a very special honour for me.

We didn't make the playoffs in 2010, but you could see the team was improving week by week. And the fans were very supportive. Bomber fans are very knowledgeable, and they sensed we were getting better. Then came the offseason.

We continued our plan to get out and meet the fans and corporate supporters in many, many communities throughout the province, and they were wonderful. Once again as I reflect on my experience with the Bombers, the interaction with the fans was so rewarding.

The 2011 season came upon us quickly. The team started well, and the fan base was so engaged, and not only on game days. Everywhere I went, people wanted to talk about the Bombers, and I never once grew tired of it. Whether it be going for walks, trips to the grocery store, or on the golf course, the fans would often approach me to offer an encouraging word. It reminds me of the Bible verse in Hebrews 10:25 about spurring one another on, offering encouragement. I think we all appreciate a word of encouragement now and then in good times and in bad. That's another lesson I learned: try to be an encourager! People in this world need to be encouraged, whether it be at work or in our personal lives. Why don't we do it more?

The momentum was building heading into the 2011 season, my second as president of the club. I wanted to see success on the field so badly for the fans; they deserved to be rewarded. We started the season very well with a win on the road and then winning our home opener. We were 2-0! We dropped our third game but then rattled off five wins in a row. The fans and our city were buzzing! And we were selling out the stadium. By the end of the 2011 season, we had sold out eight straight home games. This was unprecedented and hasn't been done since. We also broke records for merchandise sales.

Our problem went from having those empty seats in 2009 to having to add extra seats for home games in 2011. The old stadium was rocking game after game, and it was so loud. It was just so incredible. Players and coaches would often ask me during the week leading up to a home game whether we were sold out yet. The organization was working as one unit. We had developed into a tight group and were all working together. I was so incredibly proud of the efforts put forth by everyone in the building and by the players on the field.

I also remember a day when one of our employees gave me a plaque with some encouraging words engraved on it. The title was "And It Will Come." I found it to be inspirational and uplifting, and I would read it from time to time. Today, I still cherish it as it sits on my credenza in my office. It's important enough for me to share here, and I hope that in some way you can also draw some inspiration from it.

Work patiently toward the goal you've set, and it will come.

    The setbacks are no reason to quit but are, in fact, confirmation of the necessity to push forward.

    To create something of lasting value requires lasting effort and commitment. Act with diligence, with persistence, with patience, and it will come.

If you seek to get it now and then work for it later, you'll end up cheated, disappointed, or worse.

Instead, make the effort now, work patiently toward it, and it will come.

Build the value that you desire to experience, build it with each thought, each action, each moment, and each day.

Build a bright future with integrity and persistence, with faith, patience, and love.

And it will come.

A Game Day Ritual

Before I forget, I instituted a home game-day "staff get together" at the beginning of the 2010 season. I had no idea that it was going to evolve into a game-day tradition. I don't know how I came up with this, but our staff grew to really appreciate it. I need to write about it.

On the day of our home games and around the noon hour, I would ask our administrative staff to meet at centre field, and we would stand in a big circle. We could all see each other. I took a football out there with me. It was basically a game of catch with a "catch" to it. I'd start with the football in my hand and then throw it to someone, anyone in the circle. Once they caught it, they'd have to say something they were looking forward to when the football game started. Then that person would throw the ball to someone else, and so on and so forth. It was fun, and it would bind us together over time. In some strange way, this practice was a critical piece to us building trust as an office team. Yes, we often laughed, but there were times when tears were shed. As I write this, I'm starting to well up a bit. Perhaps you had to be part of this experience to know what I mean.

I can remember some of the responses. Some would say they were looking forward to a win, or Milt Stegall scoring a couple of touchdowns. I remember others saying that they hoped the mini donuts tasted good! When we'd all caught and thrown the ball and said our piece, I would ask one of our participants to "break it down," whereby we'd all come together in a very tight circle. One staff person would have the last word. Everyone would extend a hand upward and our hands would be touching. Then we'd count down together, "Three, two, one, Bombers!"

As I recall those game-day circles of sharing, I can't help but think of my last day with the organization. A staff member escorted me to centre field and shared one last time together. I found this to be so fitting and certainly very emotional.

I can still see it in my mind and hear their collective voices. I truly miss those people. What a team! This was awesome, and everyone felt part of this on game days. Great people to work with. Oh, how I appreciated this group of folks! We simply trusted and believed in one another. I think about them often to this day.

Ten

TRAGEDY, CHALLENGES, AND CHANGES

THE 2011 SEASON wasn't without its challenges, and a few of these experiences simply put the game of football into perspective. In late July, our team was preparing to face the B.C. Lions at home on a Friday night. I got word that Assistant Coach Richard Harris had collapsed in his office and that Emergency Services had been called. I made my way over to football operations and could see the paramedics working extremely hard on Coach Harris. He was lying on the ground; that visual has stayed with me. They were doing everything possible to keep him alive. The paramedic working on Richard was doing everything in his power. I remember that our "all star" defensive lineman, Doug Brown, was standing in the corridor with a few others, watching helplessly as the paramedics worked on Richard. Richard and Doug were very close, and this was hard on Doug; you could see the shock and anguish on his face.

They placed Richard into the ambulance and took him away. All of us were in shock, to say the least. We just didn't know what to say or how to react.

A short time later, I was notified that Richard had passed away. I asked my executive assistant, Deborah, to arrange to have all staff meet in the boardroom. It was at that time that I let everyone know that Richard had passed. We were all broken up by this; the boardroom was filled with sighs and tears. The sound of people weeping resonates within me as I write. The best way I can describe it is that we were all numb and in disbelief. Everyone in our building loved Richard Harris. His radiant smile, loving bear hugs, and zest for life were now gone. Suddenly gone.

You see, when something like this happens, none of us are really prepared. It can't happen to us or those close to us, right? Well, wrong. This was such a sad day, to say the very least.

A day or two later, Richard's widow, Tammy, came to see me in my office. I had no words as I witnessed her grief. It was an emotional meeting, as Tammy knew that Richard and I had a close friendship. Richard was such an encourager. There's that word again. He would come and see me frequently, and he seemed to know what I needed to hear if I was troubled by something or seemed anxious.

On the day Tammy came to see me, she asked if I would speak at Richard's funeral. She told me that this is what Richard would want, and she would really appreciate it as well. I immediately said yes. I had never done this before, other than speaking at my dad's funeral in 2002.

Richard's family had to arrange for a very big church, as there were so many people. The church was absolutely packed. There were people there from all walks of life who knew and respected Richard. The coaching fraternity is a tight-knit group. There were coaches in attendance from across Canada, and I'm sure some attended from the United States as well. Along with family, there were also many fans and people from our community there to pay their last respects.

I remember that Richard's coaching colleagues spoke, including Coach Kavis Reed, who read from Psalm 23. Coach Greg Marshall also spoke and provided some real-life stories. It was an emotional time for both these men and for everyone else. Many came from the coaching fraternity across the country. Then came my turn, and I remember I had to pull myself together after listening so intently to Coaches Reed and Marshall. I don't remember everything I said, but I spoke about the man Richard Harris I had come to know and how well respected he was throughout the Blue Bomber office and our whole community.

I needed to inject a little humour, because that's what Richard would have wanted. Coach Marshall had told some great stories that made people laugh, so that made things a bit easier. I told the story of when Coach Harris was first hired by the Bombers, and the first time I met him was in Jerry

Maslowsky's office. What a first impression! This was my introduction to the Richard Harris hug, as a handshake wasn't good enough. And the hug ended on his terms. He was a giant of a man and an NFL first-round draft pick in 1971. I remember our first meeting in Jerry's office like it was yesterday. Jerry and I were like little kids as he told us story after story. Richard had us in the palm of his hand.

The story I shared at Richard's funeral was from this initial meeting and how our friendship blossomed after that. Yes, I shared about his bear hugs. I also shared about how Richard emphatically described to Jerry and I that he was the originator of the "head slap" and not Hall of Famer Reggie White. I told those sitting in the pews that as Coach Harris described the head slap, he asked me to stand up in Jerry's office to demonstrate it to me. Well, that got a few laughs. I went on to say that I did get up as Richard had commanded, but if he had taken a swipe at me, I was in trouble. At least the guys he played against had helmets on. I think it's accurate to say that Coach Harris' memory lives on to this day. He's simply one of those people you feel blessed to have met along life's way. Just thinking of him brings a smile to my face, and also sadness that he is no longer with us.

More Tragedy

We were still grieving the loss of Richard Harris when more tragedy invaded our organization.

Approximately one month after Richard's passing, we hosted a home game on August 26, 2011 against the Hamilton Tiger Cats. Unfortunately, I do recall one specific moment from that evening. Our director of communications approached me early in the game with a shocking message. He informed me that our chair of the board, Ken Hildahl, had passed away from a sudden heart attack. I was stunned. Ken was a passionate leader as chair of the organization and thought to be in good health. It was Ken who'd called me in December 2009 and asked me to consider assuming the role of interim president. And he would be a constant encourager to me.

The news of his passing hit our organization hard. Two deaths of highly respected men within a month sent us reeling. I had high regard for Ken Hildahl, and he would be sorrowfully missed by so many.

So Close!

So much happened during the course of the 2011 season for the Winnipeg Football Club. The team started well, then struggled down the stretch; however, we managed to hold on to first place. This resulted in us hosting a playoff game, the Eastern final. The winner would advance to the Grey Cup. I remember the day of the Eastern final playoff game. Our game started early in the afternoon, I think around 1:00 p.m. I didn't sleep well the night before and got up very early. I think I arrived at our stadium by about 7:00 a.m. It was a typical November morning with a bit of a chill in the air. I decided to go for a walk inside the stadium, just to relax and calm down. It was much too early to get too excited. I remember it being so calm and cool. Snowflakes started to fall. It was peaceful and felt surreal. I remember thinking it was the calm before the storm. In four or five hours, the stadium would fill to capacity, and it would get incredibly loud. I was right.

We won the game that day to advance to the Grey Cup championship. Our fans were awesome right from the first minute through to the final whistle. My heart felt so good for the entire team, organization, and our fans. They deserved to taste victory and success. I am daydreaming about that day as I write.

Unfortunately, we didn't win the Grey Cup in 2011. We were so close, so very close. I wanted it so bad for our community, but it just wasn't meant to be.

What a year, 2011! It was the full gamut of emotions on and off the field. And there was so much going on. There wasn't an abundance of time to rest in the off-season that followed.

The Search for a CEO

I was very aware during the latter part of the 2011 season that the board of directors was going to change the operating model of the Winnipeg Football Club. I was the president, and I was responsible for everything in the front office. This included sales, marketing, finance, ticketing, and stadium operations. I had my hands full, but I wasn't responsible for football operations. I wanted that responsibility. Up until now, our general manager had been responsible for football operations, and he reported directly to the board of directors. As president I reported to the board and so did the general manager. Although I understood why this was the model at the time, I didn't agree with it. It's inefficient and can be dysfunctional. An organization needs one boss.

I agreed with the board's decision to move on to a Chief Executive Officer (CEO) model whereby there would be one true boss in the organization that reports to the board. knew it was coming; it was the right thing to do. Let me be clear. I wanted this job, and I was motivated to pursue it. I knew that showing positive results as the president would bode well for me. The search process for a CEO began late in 2011, and an announcement would come in early 2012. I brushed up my resume and applied for the CEO position. I thought I had a good chance; however, there were no guarantees.

I say I had a good chance, and here's why: We came off a very successful year both on and off the field in 2011. We hosted a playoff game and went to the Grey Cup—not an easy feat. We lost the Grey Cup game, but the organization was moving in the right direction. And off the field, we had record season ticket sales and attendance levels in 2011. We sold out eight straight games. Unprecedented. We achieved record merchandise sales for the organization. Also we made over $3 million in 2011, which again was unprecedented. The community was buzzing about the Bombers, even though we had lost the Grey Cup game.

Keep in mind that two short years earlier, our organization was in a very tough spot and we had so much work to do. I was proud of how far we'd come in a short period of time. I must also point out that we were in the process of a new stadium construction. I'm not an architect or an engineer, but as president I was right in the middle of that process. I'll write more about that as well.

Disappointing News

The disappointment of losing the Grey Cup in November 2011 was still lingering. It was less than two months later in early January 2012 when a knock came to my office door. It was our director of communications, who let me know that a couple of our board members wanted to see me upstairs. I immediately made my way upstairs and took a seat. It was at that time that I was informed that the board had made a decision.

I did not get the job as CEO. I could feel my heart sink. I knew there were no guarantees and that there would be some stiff competition, but I was bitterly disappointed. I thought I had shown enough and that the results were strong enough evidence of my leadership skills to lead the organization into the next chapter. It was a short conversation. One thing remained with me that left a bad taste. I didn't get the job, but I wasn't given any reason or explanation. Nothing. I thought I deserved at least something by way of an explanation.

The newly appointed CEO asked me to stay on with the organization. He said some very kind things, and I decided to stay on as the chief operating officer. Yes, I was disappointed, but my passion for the organization and our supportive community of fans remained. I guess you win some and you lose some. I just think it could have been handled much better. I will add that once the news broke, many of my staff and coaches came to my office to express their own disappointment. Look, I've come to know that I have my own deficiencies as a leader. I understand that. However, I will say in my heart of heart of hearts that I believe I could have done that job and done it well.

Unexpected Awards

Despite some disappointments with the club, I was also graced with a few pleasant surprises. It was some time in the spring of 2011. I was sitting in my office doing some fairly routine office work. My executive assistant, Debra, always opened the mail, and on this particular day something special arrived. Debra was wonderful at her job. I always appreciated her. She walked into my office with a huge smile on her face. She handed me a letter, and I read it immediately.

The letterhead indicted that it was from the Consumer Choice Awards. I began to read the letter and was shocked to learn that I was the recipient of the Consumer Choice Man of the Year Award. The award acknowledges companies or individuals who show outstanding commitment to customer service. It truly was an honour to receive this award. I understand that some of the past recipients of this award include Jim Balsillie, Darryl Sutter, Rick Hansen, Jon Montgomery, George Stroumboulopoulos, and John Furlong. So I was in very good company.

Later in 2011, I received a call from the Certified General Accountants (CGA) Association of Manitoba. I was very pleased to receive the news that I was being recognized for Outstanding Career Achievement. Once again, I felt so privileged to receive an award of this calibre. I had received my CGA designation in 1988, and it has been an instrumental part of my career path.

Eleven

A NEW STADIUM—WHAT A PROJECT!

The First Meeting

IT WAS IN the early years of my time with the Winnipeg Football Club when rumblings started about the need and possibility of a new stadium. After all, the stadium on Maroons Road officially opened in August 1953. By the time I entered its doors in April 2002, the place was almost fifty years old. And by the time we played our last game there in 2012, this iconic place was knocking on the door of sixty years old.

I'm almost certain that discussions about a new stadium started in earnest sometime in 2004. I was now comfortable in my role as director of finance, yet still learning. My boss, Lyle Bauer, asked me to attend a meeting devoted to the prospect of a new stadium build. I was only too happy to attend this meeting. How cool would that be?

The meeting was held at Assiniboia Downs, the well-known horse track in Winnipeg near the west perimeter of our city. Why was the meeting held there? Well, this initial meeting was all about a feasibility study to construct a new football stadium at Assiniboia Downs. In attendance were a large professional accounting firm, political representatives, some support people, and me. I was stoked!

The feasibility study was all about what a new stadium would look like, including all the amenities. I vividly remember that this study would include the idea of a retractable dome covering the stadium. For what it's worth, I understand the excitement and desire of a dome shared by football fans who live on the prairies. However, I have more of a traditional opinion when it comes to football. It's a game meant to be played outdoors, not at room temperature with no wind, no rain, no snow. Come on, do you want fries with that? I will say, however, that watching a football game on a warm summer evening with no wind or only a slight breeze is an awesome experience. I surely understood that a dome cover would significantly add to the overall business model.

The incremental revenue streams to be achieved through concerts, trade shows, and other events were all part of this potential amazing project. I was thrilled to be part of this initial meeting. I can remember heading back to the office and providing Lyle with the details of the meeting, explaining that a feasibility study would commence soon. I had an awful lot of work in front of me, but I was so motivated and inspired to do my part. I think I said to Lyle that if all went according to plan, we'd be in a new stadium by 2006, and 2007 at the latest! It's good to be excited, right?

Well, I couldn't have been more wrong. I said I was excited, and let's add humbled as well. Hey, I was only off by seven years. We wouldn't see a new stadium open until 2013, after countless twists and turns. Without a word of exaggeration, I could devote pages upon pages to this part of my career. I have mentioned the word "learning" several times throughout my career and life experiences. This would become an experience like no other. Some good, some bad.

A Marathon, not a Sprint

There would not be a new stadium at Assiniboia Downs. Simply put, the feasibility study provided that it would be far too costly, especially with the retractable roof. I also know there were some political reasons as well. Aren't there always? The feasibility study, whether it be this one or another one, also identified approximately twelve more potential locations for a new stadium. This was intriguing. At least we had options, and some locations were definitely more realistic than others. In my opinion, the Assiniboia Downs location certainly had some positives, including a rather huge parking lot. However, it was not the ideal spot—too far removed from the central part of our city. Keep this comment in mind as I add more details of this experience.

Back to the drawing board. More dialogue, more politics, more everything.

Discussion continued in the coming months and years regarding this fascinating project. Keep in mind we were also going to be planning to host the Grey Cup Game in November 2006 in a very old stadium. The volume of repairs and dressing up to be done for our old cathedral to host such a national event was significant, to say the least. This just added to our need and desire for a new venue. There would certainly not be another Grey Cup Game held at the old stadium. I'm surprised we were awarded the game in 2006.

As I recall, the momentum around the new stadium discussion surfaced again in 2007. One plan that really caught my attention was to refurbish our old stadium. In other words, devise something whereby we would remain at the current location. We were in central Winnipeg on prime property. Our fans and community had formed their niches and traditions over the years, coming and going to the stadium. Bingo! This would be ideal. Let's join hands and make this work together. Let's get our board of directors, CEO and senior management, and politicians all in the same room and make it happen. It just made a pile of good sense, again in my opinion.

Well, the dream never dies, just the dreamer. To me, this was a great idea. The challenge would be the timeline to construct. At best, if the shovel went in the ground the day after the current season ended, the project could be completed in eighteen months or so. This would mean needing a temporary home to play home games during the construction process. Complicated, yes. Achievable, yes. Impossible, no. Not without significant challenge and obstacles, but this surely made sense. I'm rambling here, as this is taking me back to that time. "We" could have done it. Short term pain for long term gain.

I remember asking Lyle for his approval, as I wanted to work on a financial plan that would either show the legitimate feasibility of building or refurbishing on our current site, or perhaps my plan would show it isn't feasible. Lyle gave me the green light, so I went to work.

The financial operating plan I put together was immense, massive. I believe the timeline included financial projections of twenty-five years, with reasonable assumptions around season ticket sales, game day ticket sales, concessions, merchandise, and all the operating costs of the organization. I was very confident in my numbers and projections. Lyle and I would review my projections from time to time, and he would often send me back to make some revisions. I appreciated him for this, as I know he was very interested. Lyle also wanted what was best for the organization long term.

There came a point in time when Lyle wanted to show our draft plan to the executive committee of our board. I was in the meeting on that day when this draft plan was presented. I was asked to present the plan, and I did so with pleasure. I knew the plan cold. I had worked with the numbers for so long that I think I could recite the plan from memory. Once I had completed my presentation, there was time for questions. I answered to the best of my ability. The one comment I will always remember came from a very well-respected member of our board who was extremely sharp. He knew the football business better than anyone in the room.

"I am intrigued," he said. He encouraged us to get on with the next steps and said that this plan should be shown to other stakeholders.

Things Get Complicated

I'm going to try and keep this next part brief, otherwise I'll just get frustrated. I'll keep it for the next book (note of sarcasm). I was informed at some point that two significant components were added to the possibility of a new stadium at our existing stadium home.

The idea of enhanced commercial retail space adjacent to the new stadium was posed. I get it. Make it a destination point. Shopping, new restaurants, etc. to neighbour our new stadium was added to the equation. I suppose the idea was meant in part to increase the level of property taxes on prime property. The City of Winnipeg would be a key stakeholder in this project, so tax revenues had their attention. I didn't like it. There was already a large commercial mall beside our stadium, Polo Park. I just felt that we were already saturated with retail in the area, so this wasn't a good idea in the big scheme of things.

The second component was to have a private owner of the football club. Say it isn't so! The Winnipeg Football Club had been a community-owned organization since day one. Leave it alone. Do not mess with this community-owned, non-profit model. The fans love the Bombers, and a major part of this is because they feel they own a piece, and they do. Bad idea!

So strike two! The idea to build at our existing site dies. I was saddened. This was a missed opportunity. I believed it then, and I believe it now. I am not alone in my thoughts.

Decision Time

Some water passes under the bridge, and I am now the president of the club. Leading the organization on a daily basis under normal circumstances was challenging enough. I believe it was May 2010 when the shovel went into the ground to begin the construction of our new stadium. Frankly, I'm not sure how the decision was made to build at the University of Manitoba. I believe I can confidently say that there were political overtones associated with this decision, to state the obvious. I believe in the end this was a project that cost in excess of $200 million—not cheap. I think the football program at the University of Manitoba was elated. They received some real benefit from having this stadium on their campus.

We marketed 2011 to be the last year of football at the old stadium. This included producing a video emphasizing the fabulous memories there over the course of close to sixty years of football. Blue Bomber alumni were interviewed and told some fabulous stories in the video. Fans participated as well. I also had the privilege to speak. It was all quite emotional.

We were wrong. This was not the last year, and frankly, I knew it long before the announcement was made that we would play again at the old place in 2012. We made two announcements. One was in early May 2012 to inform our fans and the community that we wouldn't move into Investors Field until September 2012. I think it was a few months later when it was announced that it would be 2013. Perhaps the intent was to get in by the fall. No chance.

During my time as president in the early time of construction, I made a point of having frequent conversations with my staff, the project manager on site, and even some of the subcontract workers. I am collaborative by nature. I simply wanted to keep everyone encouraged given this massive undertaking.

There came a time in the late summer or fall when I had a face-to-face conversation with someone who had a key role in the new stadium construction. He knew his stuff. I had invited him to a meeting with my management team at the Manitoba Club. We were doing some strategic planning, and of course this project was now a key component of our plans. I asked him point blank during our meeting, "In your opinion, will our new stadium be open in time for the 2012 season?"

After a brief silence, he looked at me and, for my team to hear, said, "Not a chance." I knew the truth well before announcements were made. Again, it got intensely political.

In the end, the team and community got a new stadium. We needed it. The old one had done its job, but it was getting very expensive to operate. I would say safety was also becoming a concern. I am going to repeat that the new stadium did not have to be constructed at its selected new location at the University of Manitoba. This was not the right decision on several levels. I'll leave it at that.

In short, here's what I learned from this experience. This is a massive undertaking. You need all parties working together, and I mean "everyone working together." Keep the politics out as best you can, although I acknowledge this is impossible. Political parties at all levels will likely be contributing financially to projects like this. Be honest, keep everyone informed, and get it done.

A new stadium was built. Remember I said I thought we would have a new stadium built on the old site by 2006? Ya, right, it was finally completed for 2013, and not nearly close to the existing site. The laughs regarding my prediction are on me.

I can't include all the experiences in this memoir that I endured through this whole process. I can't say that I trusted everyone involved, although there were many I did. I'm proud to know that my financial plan was in some ways part of the genesis of the project. One other thing is very worthy of mention. The first event held at the new stadium was a church service on a Sunday morning attended by thousands of people. I found it to be a very appropriate. It was a privilege for me to speak at that service.

I thought I was done with big builds of this nature. Another would follow years down the line.

A TRUE FRIEND AND COLLEAGUE

AS YOU'VE READ through some of my experiences with the Blue Bombers, you've come across the name Jerry Maslowsky. I want to focus this next part on Jerry.

I didn't know Jerry at all before joining the Bombers. My first recollection of him was in my second interview with Lyle, when I was interviewing for the director of finance role in early 2002. Jerry asked me a couple of questions, as he should. He was part of Lyle's senior management team as director of sales and marketing. It didn't take long for me to see that Jerry was very personable and outgoing. Later on, I would find out that we had much more in common. I would also find out just how passionate Jerry was about the team, and that's a real understatement.

Soon after I got the job, I started to get to know the staff better. They were a hard-working bunch who really cared about their jobs and the success of the organization. Somehow Jerry and I connected quickly. During lunch hours in the staff room, we'd get into Blue Bomber trivia, and there was no holding back. Questions about the Bombers started to flow, covering the history of the club. As a fan, I was well trained and educated in my knowledge of the Bombers, but my goodness, did I ever meet my match! Jerry's passion for the Bombers was evident in part by his knowledge. He knew player names, numbers, on and on across a number of decades. We took great pleasure whenever we were able to stump each other.

Get Jerry going on telling the story of when the Bombers lost to the Riders in the Western final in Winnipeg back in 1972 and how devasted he was at how it ended. He spoke about it like it happened yesterday. For the record, I recalled that game very well. I was thirteen years old at the time, and the Riders beat us on a last play field goal.

Our friendship started around our knowledge and passion for the Bombers. As it turned out, Jerry and I were also strong supporters of the Toronto Maple Leafs in our youth and right up to that time. The Winnipeg Jets "2.0 edition" wasn't around yet, so when the subject turned to hockey, Jerry and I were very much aligned as well.

Jerry began his time with the Bombers when he came over from radio station CJOB. The Bombers were going through an extremely difficult time when Jerry joined, so he came to the club to help out. I don't think it was meant to be for the long term, but there was no way Lyle was going to give him back! Jerry was just what the Bombers needed.

Then came game day in 2002. We all had responsibilities on game day, and mine was to ensure the 50/50 draws were organized and administered smoothly. I think it was our first regular season home game and Jerry asked me to come and stand with him on the sidelines to watch some of the game. We would stand out of harm's ways on the sideline close to the south end zone. This would be my first up close and personal experience with Jerry's passion watching a Bomber game. I can remember him doing everything he could to get the crowd to make noise when the team needed it. And on those plays when things didn't go well, let's just say Jerry's emotions were very evident with both his body language and some choice words. Jerry wore it on his sleeve like nobody else.

Our friendship deepened during our time together at the Bombers. We both felt so fortunate that we could work and get paid at a place we enjoyed walking into every day. Even on the bad days, we were still working for the Bombers.

Jerry and I worked very closely together when it was announced that Winnipeg would host the 2006 Grey Cup. This was a mountain of work but worth every bit of the climb. Jerry was such a key part of making the Grey Cup a success. I can remember a precious moment just before kickoff. Jerry and I were standing in the south endzone during the anthem. Yes, it was cold, and the stadium was already rocking in anticipation. Jerry looked at me and said something to the effect of, "We did it. This old stadium has so many Band-Aids on it (and it did!), yet it looks so good tonight. We actually put enough lipstick on this pig to make it look good for the whole country tonight." I think we shared a quick embrace. We were so proud on behalf of the whole Blue Bomber organization.

Time went on and our friendship grew. We'd often talk about family and other important things outside of football. We trusted each other. I grew to have so much respect for Jerry, and his friendship meant everything to me. Sure, there were many changes that would lie ahead within the Bomber organization, but our friendship didn't change. If anything, we grew closer as we planned to shut down the old stadium on Maroons Road and move to Investors Field at the University of Manitoba.

Time went on and we made the move to the new stadium. Jerry decided to leave the Bomber organization in early 2014, and that was a big loss for the club and definitely for me, although I understood. It was an extremely difficult decision for Jerry to leave the club he loved and had given so much to, but he had his reasons. I can remember that the club held a lunch for Jerry to honour him before he left. I was asked to speak at the lunch, and it was one of my most difficult speaking experiences. I was saying goodbye to a friend who'd meant so much to me since my first day and who had given his all to the Blue Bomber organization. I would stand up to speak for Jerry another time in the future, which was way more difficult.

Jerry and I continued to stay in touch after he left the Bombers. He had become the CEO of the Variety Club, a real good fit for him, and he was certainly kept busy. We would talk frequently and get together for coffee from time to time. On occasion our wives would join us, as Jerry's wife, Chris, and Helen had become good friends.

The Loss of My Dear Friend Jerry

Jerry took ill some time in 2016. He kept this very private. I knew from Chris that he was struggling and preferred his privacy. I got a call from Chris in late August to let me know that Jerry had to be admitted to the hospital due to intense pain. He was soon diagnosed with cancer and passed away a week later. One week!

I was shocked to get the call to inform me of Jerry's passing on Sunday, September 4, 2016. I knew he was sick, but I had no idea of the severity of his cancer illness. I was at my brother-in-law's cabin with family and friends when I got the news that morning, and I wept. I lost a very close friend, one of those people one is fortunate to meet and have so much in common with. I miss Jerry.

And by the way, Jerry passed away on Labour Day Sunday which is the day the Bombers and Riders play the Annual Labour Day Classic in Regina. Jerry was instrumental in originating that annual classic game. Call it irony, call it what you will.

Jerry's passing was felt by everyone he had touched in our community. He was one of those guys who would extend kindness to everyone he met. People warmed up to him and wanted to be around Jerry. He had a wonderful sense of humour as well. Most importantly, I know how much he cared for and loved Chris and his kids. He talked about them often.

A Celebration of Life was planned for Jerry. He met and impacted a lot of people, and an indicator of this was the attendance at the celebration. There wasn't a place big enough to hold this, so it had to be held at the Winnipeg Convention Centre. I don't remember how many people were there, but it was the largest one of these I had ever attended.

Many people spoke that night, including the "Voice of the Bombers" from CJOB, Bob Irving, and Lyle Bauer spoke as well. Chris had asked me to speak, and I followed Bob and Lyle. Listening to both of them, I was already choked up before I spoke. But I wanted to do this right, to tell people about the Jerry I had come to know. Jerry would have wanted people to laugh, so I told a humorous story or two. I know Jerry would have laughed. I know I also said from my heart that I never had a brother, but Jerry was like a brother to me. I wanted people to know we were close and that I trusted him and admired him. I believe the last story I told would have meant a lot to Jerry. It went something like this:

Although we were to play the last game at the old Canad Inns Stadium in 2011, this was delayed a year until the end of the 2012 season. We were all packing up, and our offices were starting to look cold and bare. If the walls could talk, my goodness they would have a lot to say and tell. I said to Jerry that I had an idea. I also told his daughter Tara to bring her phone and meet us out on the snow-covered field. I grabbed a football, and Jerry and I got dressed and went to the football field. It was cold, very cold. I had told

Tara that I wanted a picture of me throwing the ball to Jerry. It was the last game of catch to be played at Canad Inns Stadium.

I told this story at Jerry's Celebration of Life and added one last line: "It was only fitting that Jerry Maslowsky be the last person to catch a pass at Canad Inns Stadium. Let the record show that the last touchdown pass at Canad Inns Stadium was caught by Jerry Maslowsky."

Jerry, I miss you to this day. I miss our chats and I miss your laugh. I miss our occasional Chinese food lunches on Downing Street and Notre Dame. Rest in peace, my friend.

This my dear friend, Jerry Maslowsky on the left. I threw Jerry the last pass ever thrown at Canad Inns Stadium (December, 2012). It was only appropriate.

NEVER SAY NEVER — A RUN AT POLITICS

MY TIME WITH the Winnipeg Football Club came to an end on August 14, 2014. Again, that was a tough day. What was I going to do next? I had no idea. I deliberately took some time to try and determine my next career move. I was too young to retire and didn't seriously consider retirement, even for a moment. I think it was early in 2015 when I received a very interesting phone call.

The Member of Parliament for our federal riding, Joy Smith, was planning on retiring. She had served well for many terms. She invited me to her constituency office for a conversation. To say I was surprised to receive this call would be an understatement. I was also intrigued, although not certain as to why. Mrs. Smith and I were both members of the same church at the time, but we didn't know each other at all. She sat me down and we got to know each other a little better. The conversation turned serious. Mrs. Smith explained to me that she had decided to retire and would not be running in the next federal election in the fall of 2015. She also said she had spoken with some people, and that my name had surfaced as a potential candidate for the federal riding of Kildonan–St. Paul. As I recall, Mrs. Smith asked me to consider this opportunity and then we would speak again.

I left Mrs. Smith's constituency office that day in McIvor Mall with a whole bunch of mixed feelings and questions. I was so surprised that she would ask me to consider. I was certainly new to politics, although I follow the plight of it locally, nationally, and globally. Was I worthy of this? If I jumped in with both feet, could I possibly win the nomination to represent the party in my riding? I knew if I accepted the challenge to seek the nomination there would be a mountain of work ahead and very stiff competition.

I spoke with several people I knew and highly respected. I wanted and needed their candid views. I spoke with business people, my church pastor, and close friends. Most importantly, Helen and I discussed this at length. Was this the right thing to do, both for the community and for us as a family? We talked and prayed.

I received lots of encouragement from those I spoke to. I also got a lot of honest responses. "Jim, are you sure?" was one familiar refrain. I remember one individual I respected saying to me, "Jim, you can go into politics clean, but you cannot come out clean." That shook me a bit, but it also motivated me.

As I spoke to people, many things went through my mind. During my time with the Winnipeg Football Club, I met so many people from all walks of life. This included not just the fans but also business owners, politicians at all levels, and the media. As I pondered politics, I knew I was very comfortable with the relationship aspect. Also, I believe I had formed mutually respectful relationships with the politicians and media. That was a positive.

My experience as president of the football club was also beneficial in terms of gaining experience as a community leader. I learned that I was a strong proponent of collaborative thinking. In addition, I also tried my best to follow a servant leadership philosophy. I thought this was important too as I considered a run at the political realm. After all, are politicians not elected to "serve" and not be served?

I can remember saying from time to time in my adult years that I would "never" get close to politics. The operative word was "never." After going through a discernment process, Helen and I decided to seek the Conservative Party nomination for Kildonan–St. Paul. If you're wondering what went through my mind, I was nervous, motivated, encouraged, naïve, on and on. Never say never. I hope my decision was made with the right intentions and for the right reasons. I think it would be fair to say that I felt "called" to put my name in the ring. I knew there were no guarantees, but I was motivated to put my best foot forward.

A few things were of paramount importance to me as I sought the nomination. Remember I said that Helen and I prayed about it. As a result, I felt at peace with the decision to run. Joy Smith was extremely highly regarded as a politician. I had big shoes to fill. Jim, don't slip up, no foot-in-mouth disease! To be very candid, I had decided that if I was successful on election night, I wasn't going to Ottawa to simply occupy a chair. Please don't misunderstand me. I am a team player. I would be representing the community of Kildonan–St. Paul, and it would be crucial for me to listen to them and represent them well. I'm also not afraid to challenge within a team setting. My plan would be, should I be successful, to listen in abundance but also to make my presence felt. Respectfully, of course. Not to sound too cliché, but my goal would be to try and make a positive difference. My background is finance, and I believe in balanced budgets from a political perspective. I would certainly want to be involved in a finance capacity should that opportunity arise. I felt strong in this area. I knew I would have to become much more aware of other key political issues, such as health care and immigration and many more, as I would come to know. There was so much to learn.

I was cautiously optimistic about the days ahead. I was also new to this thing called politics. To borrow from a football term, I was a "rookie." Rookies normally are filled with excitement and energy. They have to go hard to make the team. There is joy when a rookie makes the team, but rookies can also have a disappointing outcome.

The Nomination

I had very strong competition in seeking the nomination for the Conservative Party in Kildonan–St. Paul. The other candidate had many years of political experience at the city level. His name was also very well-known in political circles. I had my work cut out for me.

For people to vote for their Conservative Party candidate of choice, they must hold a membership in the party. Once all memberships are finalized, candidates are given the list, and now it's up to them to gain their support.

I had so much help, it's hard to describe. There were people I knew who had never held a membership before, but they bought one this time to support me. I was quite overwhelmed. My extended family, my local church, and other friends and acquaintances rallied behind me. All of these people were the wind at my back. Once again, I was the benefactor of sincere encouragement, and I could feel the momentum. I gained energy from all those around me. But not every member in the riding was going to support me. I understood. I would have my opportunity to go speak with members and try to gain their support. What an exercise! You can imagine the wide and varying opinions from people regarding politics and their expectations of a potential candidate. I listened as best I could.

In early May 2015, the other candidate and myself had a chance to speak to voting members in a crowded room at a local community centre. After this, voting members would choose the candidate. I am pleased to say that I won the nomination that day. I was so excited. And I must say that my worthy competitor and I ran clean campaigns. I made it a point not to take any personal shots at him. I didn't hear any attacks from him toward me either. I found this to be respectful and refreshing.

I along with my team were again thrilled to win the nomination. A brief time to celebrate and then the race to October. There were just over five months until the federal election.

Campaigning

After winning the nomination, my work was cut out for me. I'd be up against the candidates from competing parties. And again, one of them had political name recognition. Campaigning was basically an everyday occurrence. Simply put, I was walking door to door every evening, and my purpose was twofold: I wanted to introduce myself as the new Conservative Party candidate, and I needed to listen. What was on the mind of the voters? What issues were important to them?

I also took part in a few debates, which was a new experience for me. I must say that I tried to hold myself accountable in the debates by being respectful to the person asking the question and also to competing candidates. One thing truly bothers me when I tune in to politics on television, regardless of one's political stripe. I find the debates in a legislative house or within parliament to be annoying. Add disrespectful to my list of adjectives. I'm not sure a politician has the ability to complete a full sentence without being rudely interrupted. I have often described it as an overgrown kindergarten class. These are well-paid people there to serve and work together to solve problems and move us forward. I think they all should have a hard look at how they conduct themselves. I digress.

Once again, I was supported by an incredible number of people. Some walked with me almost every night, and others knocked on doors when they could. I was amazed by the support. I was feeling good with each passing day. I was so encouraged by the responses at the doors from those who pledged their support. It's important to add that some of the most interesting and profound conversations I had were with people who clearly weren't going to vote for me. In a few instances, people clearly and unceremoniously instructed me to remove myself from their property. I can take direction! I remember one time in particular. I knocked on the door, and the gentleman (?) let me in. After a very short chat, and with his rather large dog beside him, he uttered two words: "Get out." So I did.

Let me share one more from the other side. I'll keep it short. On one particular evening, I knocked on a door, and a man greeted me. He was in his early seventies. It didn't take long to see that we had differing political views. During our conversation, he did provide his name. Let's call him Joe.

The next evening I was walking on the other side of the same street, again knocking on the doors of voters. In my peripheral vision, I could see a man approaching from the other side. It was Joe. Apparently, he wasn't done giving me his strong political opinions. I stood there and listened. When we were done our second exchange in as many days, I believe I said something to the effect of, "Thank you for your time, Joe, and have a nice evening." He seemed somewhat startled and was definitely impressed with the fact that I remembered his name. How could I forget him? I recall vividly when he told me that although he was not going to vote for me, he thought I would do well should I be victorious. I can definitely accept Joe's comments in this case. He was very respectful.

In conclusion, campaigning was exhausting at times. Helen would bake some goodies frequently for everyone to enjoy at campaign headquarters in the evenings. The campaign team grew, it seemed, with each passing day. As tiring as it was, I gained energy from the team. A special group indeed.

Election Night—An Agonizing Defeat

The campaign work was done. Now it was about the results. October 19, 2015 had arrived, and it was time for the people of Kildonan–St. Paul and Canada to speak. They would speak with their vote. Election day was like game day to me. In my days with the Blue Bombers, I tried to keep myself busy leading up to the opening kickoff. It was difficult. I could feel the anticipation and excitement of game day in my veins. Same feeling on election day.

I was sitting at home. During the early part of the evening, the early election numbers were coming in from the east coast, plus Ontario and Quebec. If I needed a hint of what was to follow, I got it. The numbers were not good for my team, the Conservative Party. However, these were just the early returns. We were only in the first quarter. Please forgive my football analogies. I can't help myself.

Helen and I made our way to campaign headquarters around 7:30 p.m. We received a very warm greeting as we arrived. I immediately made my way to one of the television sets to try and get an update, specifically for Kildonan–St. Paul. It seemed every time our results were posted on the screen, it was always very close. The Liberal Party candidate along with me were making this a two-horse race. It seemed we were always within a minimal number of votes from each other. However, I don't think I ever had the lead throughout the evening. I do remember at one point that I was within three votes. Three lousy votes.

The evening wound down and there came a time when I knew defeat was inevitable. In the end, the Liberal candidate won with 42 per cent of the vote, and I had 40 per cent. That's a close political race, but as they say, close only counts in horseshoes. I was gravely disappointed to state the obvious. But yet again, no guarantees, right?

I can remember one night soon after the election. Helen and I decided to go for a drive and grab some dinner. By the way, I love my dinner dates with Helen. I can remember sitting in the vehicle at one point and saying that I'd let people down. So many people supported my political run, and I felt terrible about the loss. I respect the political process in Canada, but losing still left a bad taste.

What Did I Learn?

I can't say this was the first thought that popped into my mind after losing the election. As time passes by and one looks back at life's experiences, hopefully we can learn something. Learn from the joyful and victorious times.

More importantly, learn from the difficult experiences. I think that learning goes hand in hand with life does it not? And if we're honest!

So what did I learn? As I said above, there are no guarantees in life (death and taxes, I get it). I worked tremendously hard during this campaign. I lost. Losing never feels good. I had experienced this in my time with the Blue Bombers. Now I experienced it again. Try to be gracious in defeat. Respect your opponent(s). Put your best foot forward, and may the results take care of themselves.

What else? Once again, although it was my name on the ballot, I learned that I thrive in team settings. It's hard for me to explain, but there's nothing like the synergy of a trusting and committed team effort.

Meeting the voters and residents in the community as I went door to door was priceless. Sure, it was tiring. I should have worn a Fitbit and counted the number of steps I took each day. I learned a valuable lesson here. It's important to respect people politically and otherwise. It's also okay to disagree. We can respect one another and disagree at the same time. Listen to people and then be heard. I didn't say this was easy. We all want to be heard. It seems to me that if you want to gain someone's respect, offer respect first by listening.

I will treasure this experience. I lost. However, meeting so many people along the way was a blessing, a true blessing.

Lastly, I remember standing with Helen one evening and looking heavenward. I felt from the outset that this political journey was something God wanted me to pursue. I looked heavenward and uttered, "I thought this is where you wanted me. Now what am I supposed to do?" It's interesting that somewhere in my soul a question resonated back to me. "Do you trust Me?" I do. I never ever thought that what was ahead for me was ever even a possibility.

Hmmm, never say never.

Fourteen

A NEW CHALLENGE — SILOAM MISSION

I Did Not Feel Qualified

THE ELECTION LOSS in October 2015 had me reeling, I will admit. What now?

I was approached by a well-known real estate brokerage. It sounded interesting, as I had never tried my hand at sales. I took the real estate courses and got my realtor's license. It's really not my area of expertise, but I enjoyed selling homes while it lasted. I did this for less than a year and was gaining some footing. I made some sales and had some things lined up for future months. Then, you guessed it, the phone rang.

I was sitting on the couch watching a Blue Bomber game on television in the fall of 2016. My wife answered the phone, as I don't like answering the phone when a football game is on television. She handed me the phone, and the gentleman identified himself as a partner of an executive search firm from British Columbia. I had met this man previously in Winnipeg, and now he was a senior "head-hunter" in B.C. Their firm specialized in hiring for Christian non-profit organizations.

He had called to say that he was in Winnipeg conducting a search for a chief executive officer (CEO) of a well-known non-profit organization. It was short notice, but he asked me if I could spare some time that evening to meet with him and another senior partner with their firm. I agreed to meet with them at the Tim Horton's restaurant on McPhillips Street.

It was a really good introductory meeting. They outlined and presented the opportunity to me over a nice cup of hot coffee and a donut. Siloam Mission was looking for their next CEO, as the current CEO, Dr. Garry Corbett, was planning on retiring. More on Garry later. I developed so much respect for that man. When the initial meeting was over, they asked me if I was interested. I believe I told them that I was, but I needed to learn and understand more about the organization. I had certainly come to know about Siloam over the years, and my understanding was that it was a well-respected soup kitchen and place for homeless people to sleep. I would certainly find out that it was much, much more than that.

The interview process continued, and I was becoming more and more intrigued and certainly more interested. However, I had no experience in working in the non-profit sector that dealt with homeless people and all the challenges associated with homelessness. As interested as I was, I really didn't think I would get the job. I just didn't have the experience, and I certainly would understand if they chose another candidate.

A Closer Look Inside

I said I was becoming more intrigued, so let me explain. I described Siloam earlier as a soup kitchen and a place to sleep, which is true, but only partially true. When I was given a tour of the building on Princess Street, I had no idea that Siloam also had a health care centre, known as the Saul Sair Health Centre. It offers up to ten different professional health care services, including chiropractic, massage, dental, physiotherapy, general doctor's care, podiatry, etc. This was incredible to see on the main floor of this old four-storey building, and it was the first thing you'd see upon entering the building, along with the old kitchen (really old!) and the dining hall that could sit up to 150 people at that time.

Then I was shown the second floor, which contained 110 beds, clean and safe, for those less fortunate to have a peaceful and comfortable night's sleep. These beds were clean and well-kept, and there were washroom and shower facilities to complement the 110 beds. It was very impressive, and unfortunately these beds would be filled to capacity every night. The third floor was mainly administrative (where my office would be), inclusive of our directors of human resources, finance, transition services, programming, and other support staff. I shouldn't forget about the office area devoted to volunteer services—so very important to Siloam! Also on the third floor was a relatively large area devoted to donor services. I would soon find out that Siloam had a very large and generous donor base.

And lastly, the fourth floor was where the transition services team would meet one-on-one with Siloam clients. Spiritual care was also on the fourth floor, and there was also an area for exercise and lifting weights. The equipment had all been donated by local businesses.

Interview Process Continues

As the interview process continued, I found myself really wanting the job. I was certainly concerned that I didn't come with the experience that could be deemed necessary, but I had also come to see that there was expertise in the building amongst the caring staff. I believed in the mission and vision statements of Siloam Mission and its core values. This was very important to me. I would say it was at the top of list in terms of why I would consider Siloam as my next place of employment.

I must clearly specify that the board of directors spent a fair bit of time ensuring that I aligned with the values of Siloam. This made sense to me, and I appreciated this very much. Siloam was founded in 1988 and is a Christian humanitarian organization. Yes, the board was interested in the skill set of their next CEO but more interested in the person and their Christian values. I agree with this priority. The leader of a Christian organization must be aligned with the mission, vision, and values, otherwise the skill set won't matter. Within an organization like Siloam, the board of directors, management, and staff all need to be aligned with the mission statement of the organization; otherwise, it will drift.

After several interviews, I got another call from the hiring firm. The senior employee in charge of this file was excited to inform me that the board would be offering me the position. I was so excited, so humbled. Again, who knew? God knew.

Let me take you back at this point to my last day with the Bombers. The last thing I did in my office was pray. I thanked God for the wonderful opportunity and privilege to be part of the Bombers for over twelve years. I acknowledged to my Lord and Saviour that I really didn't want to leave, as I felt I had so much more to offer. However, I prayed to God and asked, "Please prepare me for what you would have me do next." Was the Bomber experience my "training camp" for Siloam? My wife posed that question to me.

A New Beginning, a New Challenge

I accepted the offer to join Siloam as their next CEO, and this would commence in January 2017. This would be the beginning of an incredible journey over the next four years. I would soon find out that this was not just a job but also a very steep learning experience every day. As I will often say to people now, the Blue Bomber experience was a real gift for over twelve years. I was paid to do a job, of course, but every day I had the opportunity to walk into my passion. I was always passionate about the Bombers and the game of football. But putting things into perspective, the Bombers was about a *game* with a tremendously dedicated and loyal fan base across the whole province and beyond. Siloam, as I would find out, was about *life* at its core. There's a big difference from that perspective. At first Siloam was a job, but it became much more. In time, Siloam became a passion as well, a deeper and greater passion.

I was very fortunate that Dr. Garry Corbett stayed on for a few weeks in early January 2017 to guide me and introduce me to Siloam. As I found out, he was not only an extremely smart and wise man, but he also possessed the gifts of being kind and personable, and it was readily apparent. I said he was smart; the man has a PhD in psychology. I am not a card player, but I was never going to sit down and play poker against him! I would also find out that he could read me pretty well.

In those first couple of weeks, Garry would patiently tour me around the whole Siloam operation to provide me with a closer look and deeper understanding. I met more of the team—wonderful and caring people! He also arranged one-on-one meetings with me and each member of the executive team, my direct reports. This was such a good and necessary idea, as I got to know the people I would be working most closely with. Garry was so patient, as he could tell that although I had some leadership experience and I thrived being around people, this was all new to me. Ever have that deer-in-the-headlights feeling? Was I asking myself what I'd gotten myself into? Yes, of course!

Valuable Relationships Forming

I believe it was during my second week on the job when Garry suggested I get to know the people that utilize the services of Siloam. I was nervous. But Garry was absolutely right—it was the correct thing for me to do. I could share so many stories and experiences about my time at Siloam, and I'll start with this one.

One day early on, Garry accompanied me as we made our way to the kitchen and old dining hall. People were lined up for a meal, and one gentleman in line saw me. He addressed me by name, which surprised me. He said something to the effect of, "Hey, Mr. Bell, how are the Bombers going to do this year?" I was somewhat surprised. I decided to walk over to him, and we had a fun conversation about football. He definitely knew his stuff! He proceeded to get his meal and we left it at that and went our separate ways. This was just the beginning. I would see him a few times over the course of the next several days, and we would chat briefly. Then one day soon after he looked at me again and said, "You guys made a mistake. You should have built the new stadium where the old one was," or something like that.

Again, I was impressed. I responded with, "I agree with you, but I couldn't convince those who were making the decision to consider exactly what you're saying." We shared a chuckle, but then he made a very interesting comment. This homeless man ("John") said that he grew up close to the old stadium, which further got my attention. I told him that I did as well. One thing led to another, and we exchanged some names we remembered from our youth. It turned out that we knew some of the same people. We'd gone to the same schools, including Sargent Park and Daniel McIntyre Collegiate. I was getting more and more curious about John, as the stories were hitting close to home.

John was a few years younger than me, but you wouldn't have known it. You could see that he hadn't taken care of himself, or wasn't able to, and he looked weather-beaten and gruff. He would smile right through it; he was such a pleasant conversationalist. Finally, I got the nerve to ask him his last name, and he shared it with me. It was a very uncommon European name, but I remembered a girl in high school with that very surname. I looked at John and mentioned this girl's name, a very unique name. He looked at me with this very proud smile and said, "Jim, you went to school with my sister." John was so proud of his sister as he began telling me about her. She was married with a bunch of kids, and it sounded like she was doing well in life. And John loved his nieces and nephews too.

I went back up to my office to meet with Garry again. I should really refer to him as Dr. Corbett. It didn't take long for him to see that something was really bothering me. He asked me out of concern. I shared the story about John with Garry from start to finish, and I concluded by saying that I couldn't understand why John was there, utilizing the services provided by Siloam, while his sister was well adjusted and succeeding in life. I was having trouble reconciling this in mind and heart.

Garry looked at me and gently commented that in this life "we are all broken." I'll never forget Garry's comments. The difference was that I had a home to go to when the day was done, a home that included a comfortable bed and a fridge full of choices. Not to mention I would have a loving family waiting to greet me. John would have none of those things to go to at the end of the day. Garry was right—we are all broken (remember the song at the beginning, "If We're Honest"). Well, let's be honest then. We are all broken or have been. This is only one story of many that I could share from my time at Siloam.

I came to realize many things about homeless people. They are smart, very resilient, and wise. Two words that homeless people often say after you serve them a hot meal are "thank you."

Without exaggeration, my time at Siloam taught me that none of us is more than a day away from being on the other side of the line, but by the grace of God. It may be an addiction, job loss, or a relationship that went wrong. We all have a button inside of us that if pushed hard or the wrong way, could make us a John.

I spoke with people using Siloam's services who were accountants, doctors, other professionals, and from all walks of life. We are all broken or can become broken. To give closure to the story about John: I went home and shared this story with my wife. I remember weeping like a baby on the couch, as it just touched me deeply. I hope John is doing well these days. I don't remember seeing him much after that, and I hope that means he took some positive steps in life. I know I am pulling for him.

One last word about Dr. Corbett, as I do remember his last words to me after training me for two weeks. He encouraged me to always remember that in life and at Siloam, "It is all about service." If you and I believe in the Greatest Commandment, then Dr. Corbett is absolutely right. I know I will always remember his words.

I have so many memories from Siloam, including the "Make Room Campaign" that was established to make room for the expansion of all our services. Unfortunately, the problems associated with people encountering homelessness are not going away, and are indeed escalating. I believe in the services that an organization like Siloam provides, but society must look at ways to alleviate these problems. My journey through Siloam often had me thinking about how we can look at proactive and preventative measures rather than being reactive. I will leave it at that.

The capital campaign raised $20 million, and the donor community was outstanding with their generosity. Our levels of government were also very supportive. As a result, Siloam built a much bigger dining hall, with room for over four hundred people, and a new kitchen with state-of-the-art equipment. Other services also received a much-needed boost, including more shelter and transition beds, significant improvements to the health facility, etc. What a community can do when we work together side by side and shoulder to shoulder!

We also created a new social enterprise laundry. I was so incredibly proud when this laundry opened. It was operated by people who had previously utilized or still required Siloam's services. Their self-esteem and confidence got a huge lift when they were hired and paid a wage to operate the laundromat. It was beautiful to see. People who are down and out sometimes just need a "pat on the back," a hand up, and a word of encouragement to say, "You can do this; let us help you." Had I remained at Siloam, I would have pushed for more social enterprise initiatives.

One More Meaningful Experience

I need to share one more Siloam story, and trust me, I could share one hundred or so. Maybe that will be my next book: *Stories of Siloam*. There had been an annual event in Winnipeg for several years called the "CEO Sleepout." In simple terms, business leaders would raise money and sleep outside for one night to experience in a small way what homelessness is like. I did it, and I'll never forget it.

Siloam was asked to take over this event, and as CEO I thought it was a good idea, and so did the board of directors. We changed the name to the "Siloam Sleepout." I remember one year when we hosted, a fair number of people attended. In the middle of the night, we decided to go for a walk. We took some leftover pizza, granola bars, apples, and water to a nearby place where people were sleeping in tents—in effect, they were homeless. I was walking with a couple of young professional engineers. It was a chilly October night with wind and rain, not a night that I wanted to be outside. Note I said October. Try to imagine how people do it in January and February, night after night. Who likes being cold and damp when you can be inside at room temperature with a coffee and a sweet?

Well, our group came across a lady living in a self-made tent. She didn't have much of anything, an understatement to be sure. I think she may have had a family member or two inside when we approached the front flap of the tent and said hello. She appeared, and we had a short conversation. We made sure she was all right. She was so appreciative of the pizza and other items, we got a big smile and thank you. We knew they had to be hungry. We turned to leave, and she called us back and asked us to wait a moment. She went inside her tent and reached out with her umbrella and said, "I don't have much, but would you like my umbrella?" We were speechless. We knew we were heading back to a warm place only minutes away. We had already enjoyed delicious pizza and other items. Here's a homeless woman offering us her umbrella in the middle of a cold, rainy night. She didn't possess much more than that umbrella, I can assure you. We were humbled to the core, and I know we were choking back the tears.

Spreading the Word

I forget exactly when, but early in my time at Siloam, an opportunity presented itself. If I remember correctly, one of our local newspapers reached out to my office to see if I might be interested in submitting an article once a month. This would indeed be another tremendous challenge, as I had certainly not done anything like this in my career to date. During my time with the Bombers and with Siloam, I dealt with the media frequently. It was usually a press conference or an interview with several microphones within inches of my mouth. I always found the media to be very fair and respectful. I may not have liked the nature of some of the stories they were writing, but they also have a job to do. This is me saying thank you to all the media types I've had the pleasure of dealing with over the years. Thank you again for your fairness and your respect. Back to Siloam.

After having discussions with our board and a few others, I decided to move forward with this initiative to place a column in *The Winnipeg Free Press*. I saw it as a wonderful opportunity to connect with our community. Furthermore, it was a chance to make our donors, supporters, and community at large aware of initiatives and challenges. I had a lot of help with this, as I'm not a skilled writer. You will have noted that already! I would work with one of our senior staff people to determine a topic for a particular month, and then I'd share my thoughts with a skilled writer, and he would draft a piece for my review. I like to think it worked. I'd often hear from people who read the column, and they would ask questions, agree or disagree with any position I might take with n a given piece. I was fine if people disagreed, as it meant they were reading and paying attention to all the challenges associated with homelessness. As I look back, this was a highlight for me. Keeping a community aware with total transparency is a way to get after things together. I could feel the support of community on a regular basis; there was a real positive synergy.

Football to Homelessness, Really?

One last bit about the newspaper articles. I can remember my initial discussion with a senior employee of *The Winnipeg Free Press*. We were discussing some topics that I could potentially focus on for future columns. He asked me, "Jim, do you think there's anything transitional from your previous role as president of the Winnipeg Football Club to CEO of Siloam Mission?"

I thought about it for a second and then said yes and gave a few examples. I think he set me up, because he went on to challenge me to write a column about that very subject. (I have included this article as an appendix, and I encourage you to read it. If it resonates with you, call me and we'll talk about it.)

It was never really that difficult to find something to write about. The challenges that often lead to homelessness are numerous, and they are sad and gut wrenching. It was a privilege to try and write about this and reach out to such a caring and loving community throughout Manitoba. I tried to inform readers of the challenges people face day to day, the realities of addictions, and everything else that can lead to homelessness. I think it's appropriate to state here that I truly appreciated the love and caring spirit of the people in our communities while I was at Siloam. I learned a lot from the people of Winnipeg and throughout Manitoba. You were such an encouragement. Thank you from the bottom of my heart.

Makes Me Wonder

You know, sometimes I wonder. If we could change places for a day and learn to walk in another person's shoes before we judge them, would that make a difference? After all, we know that we all make mistakes in life, for which some pay a much greater price. I don't pretend to know all the answers. I have as many questions as you do. We are blessed with immeasurable resources in this part of the world. Are we doing enough? That's just one question.

I will always be incredibly grateful for the four years I had at Siloam Mission. I wouldn't trade that experience for anything. As I said, it was my job; however, it was a place of continual learning. It was a place of successes and failures. What did I learn? Here's a short list:

> **1. There's not a lot of difference between a homeless person and you and me.** Homeless people have feelings. Homeless people are smart and sophisticated, and they care about their community. They want to move forward in life. If you want me to cut to the chase, I don't believe I am exaggerating when I say that "we" are no further than one day away from being on the other side of the line, but by the grace of God.
>
> **2. The problems associated with homelessness are deep and complex.** There was a time when I thought that

alcohol abuse or addiction would lead to trauma in a person's life. I was wrong, as it's the total reverse. People experience different kinds of trauma and pain in their life. I trust you agree. It's that trauma that leads to drug addiction and alcohol abuse to try and numb the pain. There are days when it would bring me to my knees seeing what people deal with, and the problem is much greater in society than what we may think. I know it's getting worse, sorry to say.

3. God loves everyone. He loves and cares deeply for those battling issues that lead to homelessness. In my four short years at Siloam, I came to believe that Jesus is everywhere. He's in the bar on Main Street, and He's in the garbage bin or in the cold parkade where homeless people sleep. I witnessed these places, and it makes your heart sink. We just have to look for Him; He is present. I was so often reminded of the Greatest Commandment as spoken by Jesus: "Love your God with all your heart, mind, soul and strength. And the second is this—love your neighbour as yourself" (Matthew 22:37, 39, paraphrased)

4. People can move forward. There is no quick fix for solving the problems of those who encounter homelessness. However, I share the thoughts of many when I say it is so incredibly inspiring when you see a person's life change. It's powerful, so incredibly powerful. I've seen many come in through the doors of Siloam, utilize the services provided, and then move on in a positive light. Many times they'l come back and share their experiences. They know what others are battling, and their stories are uplifting and extremely well received. They provide hope, real hope.

5. Together we can make a difference. Once again, I have learned that homelessness and the challenges that lead to it are ruthless and unforgiving. Homelessness is a formidable foe; that is an understatement. Here's the good news: We can make a difference together. It's a monumental task, but this is a challenge we must face to help people. I know that through prayer, generosity, and working together, we can make a significant difference in the lives of many. I encourage everyone reading this to reflect on your own feelings and even judgements when it comes to homelessness. Could you imagine if all of us, regardless of our political stripe, creed, or colour, joined at the hip and decided to work at this in order to make a significant difference?

My Time Ends at Siloam Mission

My time at Siloam didn't end well. It was incredibly difficult to be candid. Without question, this was the most trying and disappointing time of my career. And if it was hard on me, it was that much more difficult for my family. Through it all, my family and closest friends found a way to encourage me, and that meant an awful lot to me. I just don't have to do life alone, and neither do you.

Let's just say there were some very trying and challenging times and circumstances at Siloam leading up to my departure. I would say things got political, both internally and externally. If you're wondering what I was feeling as I left, I would offer the following words:

Angry

Bitter

Betrayed

Misunderstood

I'm not proud to share these words with you. I am human and I had many questions. I still have questions.

As the CEO of Siloam Mission, I would be misleading everyone, including myself, if I said I didn't make any mistakes. By mistakes, I mean managerial errors or decisions I might make differently if I had the opportunity to do so. What leader is free of mistakes? It's not possible. Please know that the decisions I made were always in the best interests of the organization and those we served. I had no side agendas or secondary intentions.

I didn't want to leave Siloam Mission. I need to make that very clear. I had bigger plans in mind to try and assist people who used our services. I would categorize these plans as a "big vision." A friend taught me this term. I like "big vision," so I'm using it here. Granted, this big vision would need a lot of prayer, more buy-in from all sectors, and supreme generosity.

I want to say that I left Siloam with my principles. I know that I'm the furthest thing from perfect—just ask those closest to me. I have principles in my life that I consider to be immutable, and I trust you do as well. If we don't have our principles, what do we truly have?

I think back to my interview process when I was hired by Siloam. It was truly an honour to serve at Siloam, and I owe them a debt of gratitude for the opportunity. I gave my word to honour the foundation of Siloam. I tried and gave it my very best to serve, lead, and be an ambassador for the organization. I really did try.

Canadian Conference of Mennonite Brethren Churches (CCMBC)

At the present time, I'm employed as the chief financial officer of CCMBC Legacy Fund. As I approach retirement, I feel blessed to work in this capacity with many wonderful and caring people. I believe strongly in the mission and core values of the organization. I am committed to doing my best to serve the organization to the best of my ability until I ride off into the sunset.

Fifteen

PASSAGES

WHEN I BEGAN writing this personal reflection, I spoke about my younger years, growing up with Mom and Dad. Now I'll fast forward to the adult years. Dad and I would talk on the phone regularly. He was in his trailer home in Bow Island, Alberta, while I was in Winnipeg. Phone calls would normally take place on Sunday afternoons. We would laugh a bit, as Dad was very good natured. Our phone calls would normally end with Dad saying, "I love you," and I would respond the same way and often offer up "I miss you, Dad." Telephone calls aren't the same as enjoying each other's presence, but the calls kept us in touch over the years.

Then came a Sunday call in November 2002. As I recall, it was a typical Sunday afternoon chat. The Grey Cup game was upcoming, and Dad did enjoy football. He was very proud of the fact that I worked for the Blue Bombers at that time, about seven months into my career there. Dad appeared fine that day. He continued to battle several health issues, but he had his medications and seemed to be okay. Until the next phone call.

It was only a day or two later when I was sitting in my office. Helen called me, which was no surprise, as we would often speak on the phone during the work week. This call would be different. Helen informed me that she'd received a call from the doctor at the Bow Island General Hospital a few moments earlier. The doctor told Helen that my dad had taken a serious turn for the worse, and he wasn't sure how long Dad had left. I was shocked, feeling numb. I knew Dad had issues, but I don't think one is ever really prepared for a call like that. I called the hospital immediately and spoke to the doctor, who provided me with some details of my dad's dire situation. I asked the doctor if he thought my dad would make it until I got there as soon as possible. He expressed doubt and no guarantees. When I put the phone down, I had no idea what to do, as this situation was foreign to me.

I walked down the corridor to my boss's office and spoke with Lyle, telling him about the situation. I was emotional, and Lyle calmed me down. He immediately called our team's travel agent and got me on a flight a few hours later. Helen met me at the airport, as she'd packed me some clothes and necessities.

I flew to Lethbridge and got off the plane and into a rental car immediately. Lethbridge is about an hour's drive from Bow Island. I sped the whole way to the hospital. I had made up my mind that if I was to be pulled over by a highway sheriff, I would explain the situation and ask him to usher me to the hospital. Issue me a speeding ticket if you must.

I arrived at the hospital, and immediately after exiting the vehicle, I could see my dad's neighbour (Mary) standing at the hospital entrance. My immediate thought was that I hadn't made it in time, and Mary was there to let me know. I remember saying to her, "I didn't make it, did I?"

Mary gently responded, "You did, and your dad is waiting for you."

I made my way to my dad's room. He was unable to speak. Dad's hair was snow-white as he lay on his bed. Sure, he'd had grey hair all of his adult life that had turned white, but this was different. This was pure, pure white. Most importantly and embedded in my memory is something that happened as I sat by his bedside. He raised both his arms heavenward, as if to embrace death. I believe my dad made a decision to accept Jesus as his saviour and was now ready to meet Him.

You see, my dad was never scared of death. He would tell me from time to time that he felt that he had experienced a close to death experience when he experienced his horrific motorcycle accident in his youth. As I spent the last few hours of my dad's life beside him, I took peace and comfort from watching him raise his arms.

Dad passed away several hours later. I was beyond grateful to have had the opportunity to be there by the grace of God.

I visited a local funeral home, and they helped me make the preparations to say goodbye to Dad. The funeral was held a few days later at a church in Bow Island. Dad had a lot of friends in that town, and I think they all showed up that day. I was proud to speak about my dad and shared some stories.

It wouldn't be too long after that when I would have a "Dad experience." One that I will carry with me forever.

A Father's Day Gift in Victoria, B.C.

I am going to share a profound experience from my adult life. I say "profound" because I struggle to find the right word. Perhaps you've encountered something similar in your life. I'll do my best to clearly articulate what took place over twenty years ago.

It was the spring of 2003. Several months beforehand, my boss, Lyle Bauer, dropped by my office with a couple of free flight passes on Delta Airlines. He asked me if I'd like them. Such a kind gesture. I'd been with the Bombers for a short six months when Lyle made this generous offer. He told me to take my lovely wife somewhere nice.

This is just one of the reasons why I wanted to do my best for this man. Yes, he was my boss, but Lyle was one of those guys and leaders that I wanted to help succeed. The man was tough but more than fair. So I took the Delta vouchers with thanks and went home and shared this news with Helen. We decided to go to Victoria, B.C. We'd never been there and had heard so much about it. Fast forward to June of 2003 and plans were made. We also got free use of a condo in Victoria, so we were extremely fortunate with free flights and free accommodations. Such a nice condo too, as it turned out.

On the Saturday of that weekend in Victoria, we asked some locals if there was a nice beach close by. We were given directions to a place called Thetis Lake. Helen and I both enjoy the beauty of a nice sandy beach. We made our way there, and it was very nice indeed. Thetis Lake has a hiking trail. You can enjoy a wonderful view of the lake after you make the gradual climb. It was stunning and so peaceful. The day was filled with blue sky, warm temperatures, and a gentle breeze. Picture your perfect summer day, and this would be close.

A walking trail at Thetis Lake in Victoria, B.C. Helen and I enjoyed an incredible few days here in June, 2003. This would prove to be an unforgettable time.

I can remember making our way to the top of the hiking trail and hearing the arms of a swim club hitting the water after each stroke—quite surreal. We enjoyed every moment of the hike and the rest of the day on the beach.

However, we forgot one thing back at the condo—our camera. Helen and I enjoyed the day so much that we decided to come back on Sunday. We wanted to take some beautiful pictures to serve as memories. And by the way, both days were very sunny with nice, warm temperatures. The trip was already memorable, but it was about to become etched in our memories forever with the events of Sunday.

I must say that Saturday was made complete with a fish and chips dinner down by the harbour. It was a delicious meal with the beautiful scenery of Victoria, all the while enjoying it with my soul mate, Helen.

Sunday comes, and we make our way back to the beach at Thetis Lake. Call it Groundhog Day, as we went about our day similarly to the day previous, including the hike, but this time with our camera. As I remember, we took a bunch of pictures as we made the climb to the top of the trail.

Who Is This?

To properly describe what happened next, I need to paint you a clear picture. At the top of the trail, the walking path was quite narrow. There was dense bush on our right side as well as to the left. There was certainly no other path available to make our way down to the lake. The only way back was to reverse our steps and walk back down the path. As a matter of fact, on the left side after a few feet of bushes was a cliff that overlooked the lake.

I was walking several feet in front of Helen. I remember hearing the sound of bushes rustling, or something like that. I immediately looked right, and to my complete surprise and astonishment, a man came walking out of the dense bush. Remember, there was no path there, not by these bushes and trees. It wasn't just any man. Let me describe him. He was on the shorter side, maybe five-feet-seven-inches tall and 150 pounds. He was wearing a baseball cap as well as eyeglasses. He was also wearing a white t-shirt and had very hairy forearms and knuckles. It's also important to share that in one hand he was carrying a small bottle of pills. I thought that I was dreaming or hallucinating when I turned to Helen and asked, "Who is that?"

Helen immediately responded with, "That looked like your dad!" And that was the reason I asked. I thought I was standing eyeball to eyeball with my dad, who had passed away the previous November. You see, my dad was on the shorter side and wore eyeglasses. He would wear a baseball cap and almost always a white t-shirt. And he had the hairiest forearms and knuckles. He passed that on to me, and my kids would often joke and tease me about it. If that's not enough, my dad was constantly taking medication, and in his later years, from small bottles filled with pills. This man who came out of the bush was my dad's very likeness—identical!

He stopped for a brief moment and gently nodded but didn't say a word. I would describe the look on his face as stoic. Was he sending me a message? He kept walking to the other side of the bush toward the cliff and disappeared. Helen asked me if I'd like her to follow him and I said no. I'm not sure why I said that, but I do remember telling Helen to accept this as a gift from God.

If any experience took my knees out from under me in life thus far, this was it. I definitely had a few weak and emotional moments immediately after seeing this man. After all, it took place not long after my dad had passed away, only six or seven months previously. Although we didn't see each other often, being two provinces apart, we still spoke regularly up to the time of his passing. I missed him. Still do. This was quite the few moments, but it wasn't over.

There's More to It!

Helen and I made our way back to the beach. It was early afternoon. We enjoyed a picnic lunch and then rested on the beach for awhile. My mind was racing with what had just taken place. And then the thought came to me. I asked Helen, "Do you know what today is?" She didn't know. I looked at her and said, "Today is Father's Day!"

Coincidence? I think not. Was this a God thing, some kind of message or an undeserved gift from Him? I think so. I have no other explanation. Thank you, God, for this experience. Thank you that Helen was there with me, as it made it that much more meaningful. I'm not sure anyone would believe me if Helen hadn't experienced the appearance of this man with me.

I must be honest. Every now and then we all hear stories of some wild experiences that have happened to people. I admit to having been a skeptic when I heard them. Not anymore. I had my experience. As to why, I do not know, and I'm not sure I have to know. I am comforted to know that God is at work in my life and in yours. It's up to me to let Him into all aspects of my life and not pick and choose. I will never forget that beautiful Sunday afternoon on a scenic beach in Victoria, B.C. It was a Father's Day to remember, and I thank my heavenly Father for this precious gift.

Sixteen

GENERATIONAL TREASURES

My Kids—They Are So Precious

I INTRODUCED MY kids earlier. Their names are Trevor, Cory, and Acksanna. I hope they read this part, as it's devoted to them. If you're a parent reading this testimony to my children, then you'll understand.

Kids, when I married your mom, I was head over heels in love with her. God knew exactly whom He had chosen for me. If His command to me was to marry her, please know it was an easy command to obey.

I always tried to be a proper example for you, despite times when I fell short. I took the role of being your dad seriously. A huge responsibility comes with it, and I didn't take that lightly. It's a privilege to be your dad. A well-known saying goes, "The best thing a father can do for his children is to love their mother." If I repeat myself, it will be with the words "I love you." You've given me so much joy, and the proper words escape me.

When Mom and I decided it was time to have children, Mom was ready well before me. She cherished each of you from the moment she held you. Mom has always been a devoted, loving wife and was born to be a mom. But kids, I was initially reluctant and scared to be a dad. I confess that to you. A child needs a loving mom and dad. Becoming a dad is on-the-job training. Mom was patient as I grew to be a dad every day. I loved you all as infants and as you grew up. I love you now more than ever.

Why did you have to grow up so fast? Time does travel quickly. One moment your children are small. I blinked, and you're now mature adults.

You are still my kids. I was Dad then. I am Dad now. I will always be your dad. You are all precious in my sight.

Reflecting on these moments as your dad brings me to a simple truth that I want to repeat again and again: I love you.

Trevor

I will never forget the moment you were born. When the nurse showed you to Mom and me for the first time, you had this look on your face. I'd describe it as a look of contentment. It was like you were saying, "Nice to meet you, Mom and Dad!"

My life changed in that very moment. Looking at you in amazement and holding you for the first time is engraved in my memory. Sure, you had colic as an infant, and Mom would walk and rock you back and forth every night for hours. I think she got her ten thousand steps in every night. I would come in off the bench to help out now and then.

Trev, as I write this, so much comes to my mind. Call it flashbacks of life's greatest rewards. I know you understand, as you're a dad with three precious sons of your own.

The time came when we wanted to give you a sibling or two. You played the part of big brother so well right from the beginning. You loved your brother and sister growing up. You protected them. I love that about you. Sure, there were moments when I thought World War III was going to break out in our basement. I laugh now as I think about some of those times.

You grew up to be the big, strong, silent type. People say you look like me, and that makes me proud. Sorry if you got the short end of the stick on that one! And you have your mom's quiet demeanour; that's a Kornelsen trait. You are a true mix of Bell and Kornelsen.

Growing up, you were always so competitive. Losing simply wasn't part of your DNA, and it wasn't in your vocabulary. Trev, it was pure joy for me to coach you in soccer and hockey. You knew only one way to play, and that was to give 100 per cent whether on the ice or the soccer pitch. I loved every moment and I miss it, but I cherish the memories. And watching you play basketball in junior high and then high school was the same thing: 100 per cent effort all the time. I know you felt cheated being the shortest guy on the court, and that's because like the Kornelsen men, you were a late bloomer.

But you certainly didn't let your lack of height at the time be a detriment. I loved your character on the soccer pitch, hockey rink, and basketball court.

And we played competitive touch football together! How cool was that to play on the Eagles as father and son? I was so proud every time we stepped on the field together. And the truth is, you were a tremendous player and key part of the team. How about those "come back patterns" you would run? We were a solid duo, don't you agree? Do you remember those days when we would wear our favourite jerseys and play catch? I sure do. We were fortunate to have that big soccer field in the back yard.

I also think back to our father and son rivalry. You developed a strong passion for the Dallas Cowboys. Of course, I am the Packers guy, but we tolerated each other. I'll never forget our trips to Lambeau Field to watch your team against mine. It was so much fun to go there as a group of guys. You and I went again years later when you were early in your career as a firefighter. Do you remember the night we went for a steak dinner and sat beside a group of firefighters from Texas? They were good guys, even though they were cheering for the wrong team! I owe you a trip to Dallas to watch a game together there. How much fun would that be?

You also developed an allegiance to the Syracuse Orange basketball team. It was always fun to have you and your buddies in our basement to watch March Madness.

Trev, I was proud of you then and more so today. And of course I love your boys and watching you as a dad. Emmitt, Harlan, and Blake are so very special and provide me with immeasurable joy. I want you to know that I feel blessed in how you have always displayed your respect to Mom and me. I love you more than you know.

Cory

Where to begin? I am laughing a little right now as I think back to your time as a baby. You loved your bottle at night; you just could not live without it. And you were so bowlegged! I think the world of you. I love you! You were always the social butterfly of the family. I remember very vividly saying to people that if you ever wanted to know what was going on in the Bell household, just ask Cory!

Although you and Trev have some similarities, you are distinctly different. You have more of the physical traits of the Kornelsen men and have the Bell personality—certainly an extravert. I suppose I passed this part on to you! Cory, to share the same birth date with you (July 28) is something I will always be proud of. You were a precious birthday gift in 1987, and I am surely proud and grateful for the man you have become.

I think back to when you were playing soccer and hockey as well. You didn't care too much about the winning and the losing. You were always more interested in what we were doing after the game; the social piece was most important to you. You always wanted a friend to come over, or you would do your best to have us go out somewhere for a meal or treat. I always enjoyed coaching you too. It was so much fun, and I was proud to do it.

You inherited the position of being the middle child, the second oldest of three. That's not an easy role. Many times growing up you were your brother's accomplice when it came time to inflict grief on your sister. There were also times when you would team up with your little sister against big brother. In a sense, this was you showing your allegiance to both. I share this because you've always loved your siblings. Family means everything to you.

Cory, when you finished your post-secondary education, you served as the youth pastor at Eastview Community Church. You were so dedicated to the young people, and you gave it your all. I know the kids loved and appreciated you. Well done, son. And now to see you move on in your career and experience new challenges! Please know I am so proud of you.

And you chose a beautiful life partner in Samantha. Mom and I love Samantha very much. You have become a man with a very caring heart, and you love those around you. Like your older brother, I love you so much.

We have certainly had our share of fun together. I immediately think of our trip to New York when you and I spent a few very memorable days together. We have enjoyed so many wonderful times and share those precious memories. How about the time I got turned around on the Go Kart in Wisconsin? I know you're laughing as you read this!

Cory, I love you beyond what words can say.

Samantha, I love and appreciate you too. I remember when Cory brought you to our home the first few times. You seemed shy. As time as passed by, I loved how we joke around. You stand up for yourself very well. I consider you to be a very mature young lady. You are motivated, smart, and driven, as evidenced by your successful career as a naturopathic doctor. I know it took extreme effort and dedication to chase this dream. I see how devoted you are as a wife to Cory, and this does my heart well. I like being in your company. Please know that I will continue to pray for you and Cory as well, that God will continue to bless you with the gift of good health.

##

To all of you dads out there who have the precious gift of a daughter, you will understand my next comment. There's something incredibly special about the relationship between dad and daughter. Acksanna, you have always had me tied around your little finger. There is nothing I would not do for you.

Right from the day we brought you home, you've always been the most beautiful sight in my eyes. As I write this, I have visions in my mind of when you were just a tot, running around as your curly hair was bouncing up and down on your head. And being the youngest of three with two older brothers, you grew up tough. But you have always loved your brothers, and they loved you.

I think about the days of coaching you in soccer. What a special time in my life! You also gave everything you had on the soccer field. You were the one with the strong leg. You were always around the ball. I loved your effort, as you gave it everything. And the girls on the team for the years I had the privilege of coaching … I enjoyed it so very much. I wish we could have a reunion with all of those girls. I hope they are doing well in life.

I also love watching the relationship between you and Mom. You've always been close, and to see that loving, caring, and deep relationship does my heart well.

And how about our song, "Butterfly Kisses"?

Like your brothers, it was a privilege to watch you grow up in our home, and I am honoured to be your dad.

And now I get to watch you as a mother to your sons, Ronan and Santino. I see how much you love them and how you will do anything for them. They are special young boys and fortunate to be able to call you "Mom."

I am so happy that you married the love of your life, Nico. He's a gentleman. Mom and I think the world of him. We are so excited for both of you and your boys!

You have blossomed into a beautiful young woman making your way in life. Please know, though, that you will always be my little girl.

We have also shared some very special times. I think of coming to visit you in Switzerland while you were attending Youth with a Mission, before you went to Uganda to serve and put your training into action.

I also think of when you decided to go to school at Liberty University and how I missed you so very much. I am so proud of what you accomplished there in obtaining your master's degree.

Acksanna, you have also had to endure a very difficult time in your life. It wasn't easy. Just know that I am so very proud of you and love you with all of my heart.

Nico, I could say so much about you. From the first day I got to know you, I respected you. You are a gentleman. Beyond that, I see you are a loving husband to Acksanna and an awesome father to Ronan and Santino. I am so grateful that you came into Acksanna's life. And what a bonus that you like golf! I hope we will play many rounds together in the future. I sometimes still find myself chuckling about the fact that my daughter would marry the brother of one of her childhood friends and teammates.

May God bless your home and future as a husband and dad. I appreciate you so much and am proud to have you as my son-in-law.

To all of my children, there is so much more that I could write as the memories just flood my mind. Let's just say that by the grace of God, I hope and trust that many more memories will be made as time goes on. I sure hope so.

Thank you for the love and respect you all have shown to Mom and me from your youth until the present day. That means so much. I now know that one of life's greatest rewards is to have a loving family, and I've come to know this because of all of you, including your spouses and kids. As you know, I didn't have brothers and sisters of my own, but I sure enjoyed the view as I watched you grow up as siblings. I feel so very blessed to be your dad.

I know I have written about this elsewhere, and I will repeat it here. I imagine that one day I will stand before God, and if I'm asked what I'm most grateful for during my time and journey on earth, I will say "thank you." Thank you, God, for blessing me with a beautiful wife and three kids, their spouses, and five wonderful grandsons whom I love and adore.

Kids, as you read this, please consider doing me a favour one day. Don't assume the journey is finished. Write chapters of your own. Don't worry if it's not perfect. It won't be. Be honest with yourself and reflect. Look forward. Please remember that time is a precious gift from God, and it's unknown how much of it we get. Use it wisely; love your family and friends. Laugh a lot and love even more. Be thankful for each day.

In closing to you, I didn't get it all right as your dad. As you reflect on and recall any times where I slipped up or let you down, I would ask you again for your forgiveness. It would mean a lot. Being Dad has always been an awesome thing, and I look forward to more of it. It has truly been one of life's greatest rewards. Always remember to be there for each other as brothers and sister. I think it's safe to assume you will need each other in life. I didn't have a brother or a sister. I wish I would have had a bro or sis. I did get five siblings through marriage—a real blessing! Please don't take it for granted. Always be there for each other.

And let's make some more wonderful memories, by the grace of God. One day when I stand before Him, I will glorify Him and thank Him for the privilege of being your dad.

Special Trips with My Kids

As our kids were growing up before our eyes, I thought it would be a good idea if I got away with them one-on-one. I spoke to my wife about it, and she agreed.

The ideal time to do this was after they finished high school. Trevor would be first, of course, given that he's the oldest. Trev and I both enjoy golfing, so I planned a golf trip to the Red Rock area of Utah. We stayed in St. George, and it was a very scenic place in terms of the mountains that surrounded the area. I think we played four rounds in three days, and it was so much fun. It was a time of golf but, more importantly, a time of bonding between father and son.

We played some very nice golf courses—hard to go wrong there in terms of selection. Trevor hits the ball a lot further than me, and on more than one occasion he drove the golf ball and hit a house. On another occasion, I think he hit an errant shot into a swimming pool. We shared a lot of laughs and good meals together on that trip. And truly it was an unforgettable time. This is something I'd like to experience with Trevor again, especially now that he has three boys of his own. I can only imagine how much fun that would be.

Cory would be next when he graduated, and I asked him where he'd like to go. He chose New York—good choice! What a fascinating city, so much to do and see. And we did everything on foot. We stayed in a hotel reasonably close to Times Square and the other attractions. It makes no sense to rent a car in New York, as you can get around much easier on foot. We visited a lot of well-known attractions on the strip and also went up to Rockefeller Plaza at night. That was really neat. What a view!

I think Cory would agree that the highlight of the trip was taking in a Broadway show. We bought a couple of discounted tickets on the street to see *Jersey Boys*. They were discounted because our view would be partially blocked by a pillar in the theatre; however, we sat right near the front. The pillar wasn't much of a hindrance at all. The show was outstanding; it was the first time I had experienced a production like this, and I know we would both do it again given the opportunity.

We did so much walking in New York, and it was a great time together, a memorable time for a father and son. Sound familiar?

Time continued to march on, and it became Acksanna's time for a trip. Where would she want to go? She chose San Francisco, and neither of us had ever been there. We'd find out that this was another world-class city, and we did our best to experience as much of San Francisco in three or four days as possible. I remember the Saturday of that trip in particular. Acksanna decided that she wanted to shop. She meant it! We shopped and shopped and shopped. I said to myself at the beginning of that day that I'd go with her to every store she preferred and that I wouldn't complain. I think I kept my word, but my feet were falling off by the time we got back to the hotel. We put a movie on in our hotel room and ordered a pizza. We were simply too tired to go anywhere for dinner. I think Acksanna would confirm that we fell asleep while eating our pizza and watching the movie.

We also went down by the docks to see the sea lions and everything else, including more shops. Did I mention that the Packers were in town to play the 49ers on that Sunday? We went to the game and had a blast—so much fun.

I look back on these trips with my kids, and these are memories planted in my head and heart forever. To all of you dads out there: I know you know this, but let me remind and encourage you to spend time one-on-one with your kids. I'm not an expert, just speaking from my own experiences. Treasured memories. We have this precious commodity of time. How did I spend it? How did I spend it as a dad? I was fortunate to be able to travel somewhere with each of our kids. Many, many more memories with Trevor, Cory, and Acksanna come to my mind.

My kids are all mature adults now. All are over thirty years of age, married with families of their own. I still want to spend time with them. They are fun and worth every second. I love them deeply and treasure my time with them. As I reflect, I wish I'd spent more time with them. I'm not complaining. It's just that they're worth it, every minute. Come to think of it, I still can.

Being a Grandparent—What a Blessing

As parents, I suppose we all wonder at some point what it would be like to be grandparents. I only knew one of my grandparents, and that was my grandma on my dad's side. My Grandpa Bell died when I was just a little guy. I think I was three or four years old. I've been told that I take after him.

I never had the pleasure of meeting my mom's parents. My mom's mother died when she was very young. Although her dad lived into his nineties in Ireland, I didn't meet him.

But now I am a grandpa myself, and it's one of life's greatest rewards. Helen and I have five grandsons. It's a wonderful time of life. I enjoy spending time with all of our grandchildren. They are such a blessing and fill my heart with joy.

The names of our grandsons are Emmitt (twelve), Harlan (nine), Blake (six), Ronan (five), and Santino (two months). What is it about them that I enjoy the most? I just love being in their presence. I like the way they call me Grandpa or Pappa. It just feels good. I also take joy in listening to them tell me their own youthful life stories. They generally involve what's going on at school, the hockey rink, the soccer pitch, or the baseball diamond. The four oldest have stories to share, and I find them to be compelling. I'll have to wait to listen to Santino. For now, I'm more than content to hold him and look into his eyes. What goes on in the mind of a two-month-old anyway? I always look forward to watching them play on their sports teams. One of the things that Emmitt, Harlan, Blake, and Ronan share in common is that they have very competitive spirits. I like that. I was the same way growing up.

I realize that time doesn't stand still. These boys will grow into young men before I know it. I look forward to spending more time with all of them in the days ahead.

I want to be a good grandpa. What does that mean? I want to continue to be there for them when they want to talk to Grandpa. And I want to listen. They have lots to say. Frankly, I think I can learn a lot from them. In return, I may have some advice for them from time to time. I'll offer it up when it's appropriate.

One thing for sure: I am praying for these boys. If Helen and I are to be blessed with more grandchildren, we will pray for them too. After all, they are a blessing received from God. To each of my treasured grandsons, the following is a personal note to each of you.

Emmitt

You are my first-born grandson. It's hard to believe that you're twelve years old. You are a pure joy and so much fun. I enjoy every minute of our time together. I remember those days when you were three or four years old and your favourite thing to do was to lie on the floor and play with your Hot Wheels. How about all the times we would play mini sticks in the basement? As you have gotten a bit older, your interests have evolved. You've developed such a passion for sports, specifically hockey and baseball. It looks to me that your mom and dad have passed on their competitive nature and talents to you. Emmitt, I love watching you play on your teams. You always give it your best. It's such a privilege to watch you. I am so proud of your effort. Never lose that desire to give your best; it will serve you well as you get older.

You remind me so much of your dad when he was growing up. I would encourage you to keep doing the same thing on the baseball diamond and on the hockey rink. Do your very best at sports and commit yourself to that same attitude and energy in the classroom at school. Always remember how much your parents love you. Please stop and think about all that they do for you. They do everything for you and your brothers because they love you very much. They only want what's best for you. Take the time to tell them that you love them. Always respect your parents, even when you might not see things the same way that they do.

Emmitt, I'm not sure when you'll have a chance to read this, but I hope you get an opportunity one day. It won't be long until you're "all of a sudden" a teenager. Continue to develop good habits and make good decisions. You'll find as you grow up that some things you will face will be challenging. I encourage you to always do the right thing, even if some others are leaning the wrong way. You will likely encounter pressure from those your own age to do things that aren't wise. Try to surround yourself with friends who make good and wise decisions.

You are also a tremendous example of a big brother to Harlan and Blake. Keep it up, Emmitt. Grandpa loves you.

##

What a special boy! The first thing I remember about you is how much I liked your name, and it really suits you. Like your brother Emmitt, I can see that you are very competitive. I can remember when you were a little younger that you always wanted to play mini sticks with Grandma and me. As I watch you grow up, I see that there's something special about you. You are extremely competitive like your brother, and you have a very kind heart. I watch you play hockey and baseball, and I can see your leadership skills developing. When I sit in the stands at your hockey games, I often say to myself that you are a coach's dream. Your effort is outstanding, and you're always the first guy back to take care of your end of the ice.

And you love to play the game of UNO, sitting around the kitchen table at our home or at the cabin. You sure like to beat Grandpa at UNO and other table games, don't you? The other thing I notice is that you always keep score. You are so good with arithmetic. Keep it up, Harlan!

Harlan, as you grow up, the world will need strong male leaders, men and people of principle. If you're blessed to be a leader in sports, at work, or in the world, it's my hope and prayer that you be strong and courageous. Surround yourself with loyal and trusting friends. And like I said to Emmitt, always love and respect your parents and be the good brother that you are.

Harlan, I look forward to the coming years to watch you grow into a fine young man. Always know that Grandpa loves you very much.

Blake

Oh Blake, the youngest of the three Brandon brothers. As I write this piece, you are now six years old. I know it can't be easy growing up as the youngest of three competitive brothers in the same house. Like your brothers, you are so special to me. So far, I haven't had the same opportunity to watch you play hockey like your brothers, but I do look forward to it. One of the things I do know is that you like to ride your little motorcycle!

Blake, as I observe you, I can see that you have a very kind and caring spirit. That's a gift. I hope this stays with you as you grow up. One memory that stays with me was one day when we were skating in the back yard with your brothers. Grandma didn't have skates on, and you reached your hand out to help her walk across the rink.

Blake, I also think of the time we went horseback riding at Falcon Lake, and you loved it. You also like to play mini-golf and go for ice cream when we enjoy so many good times together at the cabin. I look forward to spending more time with you and creating more precious memories together as you grow up.

I also hope that you will always do your best in school and give it your very best effort.

I also want to encourage you to love and respect your parents. Listen to them. Blake, like your brothers, I love you very much.

Ronan

Ronan, up to very recently, you were the youngest grandson, and now you're a big brother. You are fast—very fast. I see that firsthand when you play soccer. I enjoy watching you play. And now you're in school, a sign that you're growing up. I understand that your teacher in school says that you are a peacekeeper and you enjoy being with your friends. I encourage you to remain a peacekeeper as you grow up; those around you will appreciate this about you.

I also see how much you love your mamma and Nico. Like your cousins, I encourage you to continue to love and respect them as you get older. I know they both love you very much. Ronan, as I write this, you have recently become a big brother to Santino. I see how you care and watch over him in a kind and loving way. I look forward to seeing how you teach him to play soccer when he gets his legs under him.

On those nights when we have sleepovers, I like it when we sit on the couch together and read Bible stories. I hope we can enjoy more of those.

Ronan, we've enjoyed some special times. I have always enjoyed walking or riding on our bikes to the park with you when you come for a visit. And just like Grandma and your cousins, you sure like going for ice cream. I have always loved it when you come watch my football games, wear your red #4 jersey (same number as Grandpa!), and run around with the guys before the game. You're part of the team!

Like I said above, you are fast and you like to run. I encourage you to run the race of life well. Choose wisely and make good decisions. I love you, Ronan.

Santino, how I love your name. I understand your nickname will be "Sonny," and I really like that too. You are so new to this world. I love holding you and looking at you, wondering what the future has in store for you. I look forward to spending time with you and creating some special memories. Like your brother, Ronan, and your cousins, you have won my heart already.

I feel as though I should write so much more about Emmitt, Harlan, Blake, Ronan, and Santino. For anyone reading who is a grandparent, you will understand when I say grandchildren are treasures. They are the rich rewards provided by a loving God.

A precious memory that includes all five of my grandsons took place recently, in August 2024. Our whole family rented a pontoon boat at Falcon Lake on a beautiful Sunday afternoon. We spent over three hours on the water together in the boat, and we also went fishing and swimming. My son Cory prepared a video of that special afternoon. I will never forget that day with my five grandsons.

My precious grandsons (left to right, Blake, Harlan, Ronan, Santino and Emmitt), August, 2024.

This is Us, all of us on a beautiful Sunday afternoon in August, 2024. We enjoyed a beautiful Sunday afternoon on the water at Falcon Lake.

Boys, Grandpa will continue to be around you and support you as much as I am able. I will watch your games, cheer for you, and listen to you carefully when you have questions for me. I commit to praying for you, that God will provide you with much wisdom and guidance as you grow up. As brothers and cousins, I encourage you to always be there for each other. I love you all more than words can tell.

Remember, always respect your parents. The Bible says , *"Honor your father and your mother ..."* (Exodus 20:12a).

Seventeen

HELEN — MY BEST FRIEND AND SOULMATE

HONEY, I WROTE a fair bit about you earlier, but I'm going to do it again. You have endured forty-two years of marriage with me, so I think you deserve to be written about and acknowledged! At first it was your smile, your curly hair, and shy way that won me over, and then it was your heart. You were my eye candy then and now. And then I got to know you a little at a time, and I fell hard for you. The truth is, I love you more with each passing day.

Sometimes I'd hear someone describe their spouse as their "soulmate," and I would wonder what that meant. It sounds so endearing. I looked up the definition, and one version says that it's "a person who is perfectly suited to another,"[1] as in a close friend or romantic partner. And you are just that — my soulmate. You are so ideal for me, and I believe we are ideal for each other yet with so many imperfections. Mostly mine! You are my best friend. I want you to know that it's my privilege to have you as my wife for this journey of life.

To have you as my wife for life's imperfect journey has been my life's greatest privilege. Every now and then I tease you about a song. The song is by The Carpenters ("Close to You") and a line in it talks about the angels getting together and creating "a dream come true." This reminds me of you.

We share so many precious memories. We've also endured life's challenges together. I pray there are more rich

---

[1] *Merriam-Webster Dictionary*, s.v. "soulmate," accessed September 18, 2024, https://www.merriam-webster.com/word-of-the-day/soul+mate-2016-08-15.

experiences ahead that we can share together. Sometimes just the two of us. Sometimes together with our kids and grandkids. And sometimes with our dear friends.

We prayed together on our wedding night and asked God to be part of us, to be in the middle. He answered. Thank you, God.

The Last Chapter

—OR IS IT?

AS I PEER into the rear-view mirror, reflecting on the pages of my life, I've wrestled with how to bring this memoir to its conclusion. The question has echoed in my mind: "How do you craft the final chapter of a life still unfolding?" But then a realization struck me: this life journey isn't concluded here; it's an ever-unfolding narrative.

So let's embark on a different ending together, if you will. If you've journeyed through my life's stories, in whole or part, I'd like to extend a loving challenge your way. You see, I've come to believe that each of us is an author in our own right, chronicling our unique stories every day. Whether you put pen to paper or simply live, you're an author. Respectfully, I don't think you can argue that point. You're an author. And herein lies my challenge, for in sharing our tales, we find connection and profound meaning.

Indeed, life is an unpredictable voyage, a continuous story scripted with each sunrise and sunset. As I've engaged in this writing exercise, I've found it to be a deeply enriching experience. By sharing my own experiences and the lessons life has bestowed upon me, I hope to ignite a spark within you to do the same. Yet a profound realization has settled within me: My memoir will never truly be complete. I know that sounds like an odd way to finish this exercise—incomplete. But I do think it's appropriate. The future remains veiled in uncertainty, its pages blank and waiting. What I do know is that each tomorrow is a gracious gift from God, a fresh opportunity to script more chapters. More challenges to overcome, more opportunities to seize, more unique experiences to cherish. Let your stories be a legacy for those who come after us, a testament to the beauty of our shared existence.

So building upon the challenge I extend to you, my cherished family and friends, may you journey onward every day with the awareness that you too are authors of your stories. Embrace your personal voyage, challenges and all, with open hearts. And remember, you need not journey alone. Venture forward with loved ones and dear friends by your side, for their presence makes the story richer. Most importantly, I invite you to invite God into your journey. He created you and me. I know this—if you invite Him in, He loves you so much that He will accept your invitation immediately.

Please consider this memoir incomplete, for I've come to find solace in that thought. Life's journey is meant to be an ongoing, ever-evolving narrative. My prayer for each of you is that you discover the same love, strength, and inspiration that have carried me through mine.

Now I feel the urge to celebrate with a walk, a conversation with Jesus. He has been my constant companion on this winding path, so a walk with Him is more than fitting. But before we part ways, allow me to leave you with this profound question: "Do you have room in your heart for God to write His story?"

Afterword

TO MY FAMILY AND FRIENDS

I MUST ADMIT that this attempt at writing has been an incredible personal experience in several ways. I would be honoured if my family and friends have an opportunity to read about my life's experiences. I want to share it with you because you have shared yourself with me.

I hope that you get a feel for how much you all mean to me. If not, then I have failed in getting my message across. If you are in fact reading this, I do apologize for going on at length in certain areas, perhaps even repeating myself too often. As I have reviewed everything I have written, I can certainly see many flaws in my writing skills, but this was never meant to be a piece of literary perfection. I could never achieve it. On the contrary, I hope as you read that you will say that this is all part of "Jim being Jim." All part of a very imperfect journey. My life has not been perfect. I am far from it, and so are my writing skills!

But please know that f you are mentioned, it's because I love you and you mean so much to me. Some people are in here by name. Some are not. I certainly didn't mean to offend anyone if your name isn't included. You have been, and many of you continue to be, so much a part of my life. I am so very grateful for each of you. You may have read that I thanked God for His patience with me. I extend that thank you to all of you as well, for your patience and tolerance. I know I have tested many of you in this regard from time to time! I must say that sometimes I really enjoyed poking fun at many of you and getting under your skin in a playful kind of way. That's just my way of saying that I enjoy your company. I don't think this will stop. I can't help myself.

On a much more serious level, I firmly believe in my heart of hearts that the day will come when I stand before God and give an account of my life. We all will. I have said on occasion to Helen that if we are in that line together in heaven and should I be in front of her, she should go for a coffee. I think I'm going to be there for a while!

If I am allowed to speak in God's presence, I will thank Him for the privilege of knowing you and doing life with all of you. Some of you are family and some are dear friends. Let me contradict myself—I consider many of you to be family, even if not by blood or through marriage. If I proclaim here that I am indeed so grateful for all of you, it seems to me that I should tell Him when given the opportunity.

By the way, I wonder what heaven will truly be like. Some days I think about it. Once I'm there, I hope to speak to a few people mentioned in the Bible as well as many people who have gone before me. Well, more than a few, but the first ones I would seek out would be Daniel and Barnabas. Why? you ask.

The Bible is an amazing book, and I have a few favourite parts. People in it have spoken to me in a very meaningful way. Let me share a couple of examples. The book of Daniel is one of my favourites. It always astounded me how this young man and his group of three friends remained steadfast in their respect and obedience for God. Daniel's discipline was truly unwavering, and I have so much respect for him. I would encourage you to read this short book in the Old Testament. You can read it all over one cup of coffee, maybe two.

And then there is Barnabas. Who wouldn't want to hang around with a guy known as the "Son of Encouragement"? There's not a tremendous amount written about this man, but enough to know that I would like to have some of his attributes. We could use more guys like him today, couldn't we? I hope it's appropriate here to challenge us all to be encouragers.

I believe God gives many opportunities every day to be a sincere encourager. Let's accept the challenge! The world needs more people like Barnabas. May it be that the Barnabas in you and in me will shine brightly in a world often surrounded by darkness. May God bless you for it.

As I dare to look forward, I hope that I can experience more of life with you. What do I mean when say do "more of life" with you? Let's keep meeting together. Let's keep serving together. Let's keep playing touch football together. Guys, when is our next game? Let's do church together. Whether we attend the same building or not, we can still do church together. Let's keep golfing together. Let's laugh and cry together. Let's put all our imperfections together and see what we can do … together. I will say it one more time—I have come to know that we are not here to live life alone. Let's use our time wisely; it is a precious gift. Now I am reminded of one of my favourite scripture passages in the Bible:

> And let us consider how we may *spur one another on* toward love and good deeds, not giving up meeting together, as some are in the habit of doing, but *encouraging one another* – and all the more as you see the Day approaching. (Hebrews 10:24–25, emphasis added)

I am truly inspired by the phrases *"spur one another on"* and *"encouraging one another."* There's something about the verb "spur" and the command to "encourage." Let's accept the challenge.

If you want to know my second verse, it reads like this: *"Gray hair is a crown of glory"* (Proverbs 16:31a, NLT). Ha-ha, made you look!

My Hope

To wrap this up, there are a few things I hope for.

I hope you enjoyed reading this. I hope you laughed. Maybe you shook your head in places because you disagreed with me or maybe thought I was off my rocker. Maybe you're familiar with some of my experiences, while others you're learning about for the first time. If you're reading this, it's likely because you know me pretty well, and I hope you know me even better now. And I understand if some or most of what you read wasn't that exciting or glamorous. I get it.

I hope you and I have many more experiences to share as we journey through. I would be honoured to share more of life with you.

And my greatest hope and encouragement to all of you would be to get to know this loving and gracious God if you don't know Him already. Please know that He loves you very much, more than words can express. Life without Him may seem fulfilling; however, I would encourage you in the most loving way to get to know Him. Invite Him into your life. I am reminded of a Christmas song that tells a beautiful story but also challenges the listener with a question: Is there room in your heart for God to write His story?

I think the lyrics of the song point out a question we all have to ask ourselves. Just being honest! Feel free to hold me accountable to the lyrics. I want and need to leave room in my heart for God to write His story. It would be a great book to read one day if we all left room for Him to write. It won't be perfect, but know that grace and mercy make for a great theme and ending.

I'd also encourage you to pick up a Bible, and don't worry if you don't understand it all. Leave your heart open to its message. I promise you, it's worth the read. Get to know this God and His Son, Jesus. If you're wondering how else to get to know Him, just ask Him to make Himself known to you.

Imagine yourself sitting at the feet of Jesus. It's the greatest gift I can encourage you to pursue. Who else do you know who would love you so much that He would hang on a cross and die for you? He created us to have fellowship with Him and with each other.

I also hope you are blessed as you experience the rest of your life's journey. It won't be perfect, to be sure. But it's worth the ride with people like all of you.

Remember that every day is truly a gift, and may we all use the time wisely. Don't travel life alone, and as a man once said to his son, "Make every day your masterpiece."

God Bless you all.

A NOTE TO GOD

I HAVE CHRONICLED many of my life experiences, realizing that imperfections may have caused unintentional omissions. It's part of being imperfect. Throughout this endeavour, I've pondered what I've learned, whether certain episodes were mere anecdotes or held deeper meaning. I believe some experiences are meant to shape us, and I've often prayed for God to chisel away at me. Underneath it all, as I age, there's a growing desire to chase the character of Jesus, acknowledging that God has much sculpting left to do.

Reflecting on what I've written, it becomes evident that the central theme is relationships. It's an ode to the wonderful people God has placed around me—a gift I'm grateful for but perhaps take for granted at times.

I pause to express gratitude to God for these treasured relationships, both family and friends. Thank you, too, to those who've walked alongside me graciously, teaching and influencing me. By God's grace, He has surrounded me with caring individuals. As I conclude this memoir, it seems fitting to write a personal note to God. While I can't repay Him for the grace and love He has shown me, I want to express my feelings.

> Dear Lord,
>
> Embarking on this writing journey without a plan has taken longer than expected, but I'm grateful for the reflections. Thank you for your immeasurable love and grace, for always being present even when I didn't realize it. Your

answers to my prayers haven't always aligned with my expectations, yet you've been consistently faithful.

I've learned the importance of speaking to you more, of praying more. I need to do more of it. Your infallible Word, your faithfulness, love, and grace have become even more evident to me. Thank you for your patience during moments of my youth and adulthood when I tested it.

Psalm 51:10a resonates with me: *"Create in me a clean heart, O God"* (NLT). I submit it as my prayer. I strive for a clean, pure, and spiritually healthy heart that honours you. Recently, I read a book emphasizing the importance of a healthy soul, where will, mind, and body are in sync. Help me, Father, achieve this harmony. I want to preserve my spirit, soul, and body complete and in line with your teachings.

I've been blessed throughout my journey, especially with wholesome and loving relationships. My imperfect path, when distilled, echoes a theme—life enriched by meaningful connections. Even as questions remain unanswered, one truth prevails: true and wholesome relationships are invaluable.

Time, a precious gift from you, has become increasingly significant as I age. I aim to use it wisely, adhering to the Greatest Commandment—to love you with all my heart, soul, and mind and to love my neighbour as myself.

Thank you for the incredible people you've placed in my life, especially Helen and our children and grandchildren. They are gifts beyond measure. Lord, I can't repay you, but I commit to being your servant, trying to walk daily as your ambassador and apprentice. With all my imperfections, I submit myself to you.

APPENDIX I

THE FOLLOWING WAS written and contributed by my very close friend and Knights teammate, Sean Lehmann.

Jim has asked me to put together a couple of thoughts to insert into his upcoming memoir. Seeing as I've known him for over thirty years, played hundreds of games of football and golf with him, gone on family vacations together, watched each other's kids grow up, and gone to family weddings and funerals, I'll do my best to paint an accurate picture.

I don't remember the day or the game, but I probably met Jimmy for the first time by playing touch football against him. Those days I was floating from team to team, just trying to play football as much as I could, and I would be put on a team with other "single" players. At some point my patchwork team would play against the Eagles, a well-known, family-based team that had been playing together for years and even at that time was a well-oiled machine. They had Jimmy at QB, Jake leading the scoring, and Henry calling defence. They easily put down our team of individuals and showed us how the game was played. I knew at that time that I wanted to be part of this type of team.

After getting our clocks cleaned playing against the Eagles in the Golf Dome one night, I approached Jim to ask if I could play on the team. What happened next depends on who you believe. If you ask me, Jim game me the side eye and said, "I think we're good, and maybe I'll talk to the other guys and see if we need an extra guy." Years later, Jim claimed that he was excited to have "red sweats guy" join the team (I habitually wore red sweats in those days), and he even recruited me. Regardless of how the decision was made, I made it out to practice that spring, and after running back the opening kickoff for a touchdown in the first game, the rest was history.

The next thirty years or so are a little bit of a blur. We prepared every week in the summer, gearing up for our weekly game against another powerhouse team in Manitoba. We were in more provincial finals than I can count, and often Jimmy would lead the team to victory, with the Eagles taking their fair share of provincial titles. Win or lose, we would often go out for dinner with the team and family, who were at all the games, with the kids playing their own childhood games on neighbouring fields and picking the restaurant we would go to. It was during this time that I felt I was fully embraced by the group, and we started playing golf and floor hockey together, sharing Friday morning breakfasts, and travelling for football and vacations. We bonded during the good times and became family during the bad.

I've always considered myself a bit of an outsider to the group. The group, all their family and friends, have a deep sense of faith that I don't possess. Despite this difference, the group welcomed me and my family with open arms and took me in, warts and all. I suppose upon further reflection we're not all that different—we all have a strong sense of family, connection to community, drive to do the right thing, and desire to be accepting to people and groups that are different than us, mixed with a strong sense of humour. Maybe that's how I got in. Regardless, I'm grateful to be included.

I think we also all share the same opinion that this group of men is special and that the relationships we've created and maintained over the years are very valuable—at least they are to me. It's never lost on me that this situation is unique and rare and needs to be respected and protected. I have countless examples in my life where people, especially men, don't have this type of support system in place and have never known this level of support. Everyone in the group knows that whether you need a fourth for a tee time, or you need a garage built or some life advice, we have this group we can lean on and be there for us in both the good times and the bad.

I would be remiss at this point not to mention Jimmy's playful nature and pathological need to trash-talk during golf games or any other competitive activities. Don't get me wrong, it's always good natured and harmless, and he can dial it down before things get heated, but it's always in the background. Things like standing over the tee of a four-hundred-yard par four and saying, "I think I'll layup on this one." Being ten strokes behind on the final hole and out comes "The seventeen practice holes are over; this one is for all the marbles." Whenever he's trailing in a game, he's "right where he wants to be," and the classic "don't care if the horse is blind, load the cart!" No one knows what he's talking about, but that's the whole point. Whenever he took the lead or was doing well, the trash talking would subside and he would be a graceful winner ... for the most part. My theory is that because Jim didn't have siblings, he didn't get beat up when he started trash talking and has never discovered healthy limits. Just a theory.

When I think of Jim, dozens of stories jump to mind. I call them Jimmy stories. A typical Jimmy story is one where Jim has done something odd or absent mindedly and made himself look like a fool; however, he doesn't see it that way and plays himself as the victim or claims he is being targeted. There are far too many to document here (maybe the next book), but here's a small taste.

Jim comes home with a couple of pizza boxes for family dinner, but when they open the boxes, they find all the pizza slumped to one side. "Did you get in a car accident on the way home?"

Nope. Maybe it's just one box, so they open the other and sure enough, the entire pizza is crammed to one side. "We should call and complain," says Helen.

"Dad, what did you do?" asked Cory.

"Nothing. I was carrying the pizza normally to the car, had to get the keys out of my pocket"—he motions that he took both pizza boxes, turned them sideways, and pinned them under his arm to fish the keys out of his pocket—"Oh, maybe it was me."

"The pizza still tasted good," is Jim's only response.

Another key attribute I will always connect to Jim is a sense of resilience. Whether he's navigating new leadership at the Winnipeg Football Club (Blue Bombers), running politically for Member of Parliament, or a target of character assassination at Siloam Mission, Jim will keep his head, be slow to anger, and always have a measured and restrained response. That combined with his sense of faith and family truly paint a picture of who Jim is.

I've always looked at life like a game of football. You can look back on a game of football and identify key plays that turned out to be critical. If the receiver would have caught the ball, or if the defender hadn't gotten a penalty, the game would have been different, impacting who won or lost. Looking back on my life, meeting Jimmy and being involved in the family football team was a critical event in my life. I value my relationship with Jim and the Kornelsens, and I'm thankful things worked out the way they did with our families coming together and having each other in our lives.

APPENDIX II

What Do Football and Homelessness Have in Common?
BY: JIM BELL, SILOAM MISSION CEO

MORE THAN YOU might think. Let me explain.

In my days working for the Winnipeg Blue Bombers, I would often see our coaches scheme for the next game by studying the opponent.

Armed with a whiteboard and footage of past games, they would analyze how much of a nuisance the opposing linebackers might be. Maybe how to deal with a particularly fast wide receiver. Or how to best block an aggressive pass rusher in order to protect our quarterback.

They identified gaps and built plays around exploiting the opposing team's weaknesses. And they prepared a strategy to put up a rigorous defence against the other team's strengths

This prep work was crucial to have any chance of success on the field.

In my current role serving our city's vulnerable population, I'm reminded of what those coaches taught me about knowing what you're up against.

Except this time, our opponent is homelessness. And when we put it up on the whiteboard, it looks like a grueling task.

Just imagine that the defensive line we are up against is addictions. When you try to move people down the field who come from a background of trauma and you come face to face with alcoholism and substance abuse, you better have a game plan.

And if you make it past addictions, you then have to face the linebackers who represent relationship fallout and a history of abuse.

And if that's not tough enough, you look around and notice a secondary dominated by mental health illness.

Suddenly you realize that you're up against an unfair opponent. You don't know where the blitzes will come from, and you have no idea how to game plan for the unexpected.

You can be doing well with just a few yards to go when all of a sudden, a bout of debilitating depression hits you out of nowhere.

Maybe you have just intercepted a bad situation and are heading in the right direction again. The wind is at your back. Your team is stout.

Then, without warning, you take a blind side and spiral into relapse.

No matter how you look at it, homelessness is a brutal, unforgiving foe.

But there's hope.

Like the Blue Bombers, our efforts to end homelessness in Winnipeg are owned by the community. And we have some of the best fans and supporters in the country.

In football you're only allowed 12 men on the field. But when it comes to helping the city's vulnerable men and women, there's always room for one more. And we need all the help we can get.

Right now, we're still in our own end of the field and making progress. The hard work that has been done in our city by so many groups over the last three decades has given us a few first downs and the confidence to move forward.

But our opponent is gaining momentum.

And the only way to beat it is to help one person at a time get into the end zone.

That means transitioning people into housing models that provide the critical supports to help with their recovery. It also means helping them develop soft and hard skills that allow them to take part in our society.

And when we get them there, we celebrate the touchdown with them. Then we humbly turn around and move down the field again for the next one.

This isn't training camp; it's game time. We have an incredible opportunity, and the ball is in our hands. I know we can win, but we need to rally together as a community to do it.

Originally published by *The Winnipeg Free Press*

APPENDIX III

THE FOLLOWING WAS contributed to my memoir from Owen Kornelsen. Owen is my nephew and teammate on the Knights.

As I was growing up, two things were pretty much set in stone for me: working in the family business and living and breathing football. Initially, I found myself more drawn to the friends and family on the sideline than the game itself, but soon enough, I caught the football bug.

Things started to change when I watched my older brother, Jeremy, and my older cousins team up with their dads. Unsurprisingly, I found myself in love with the game too. Every season felt like my last chance to play with my dad and uncles, so I poured my heart into each match. Strangely enough, it's been a whole eight years, and they're still giving it their all. Their unwavering commitment to the game has been truly inspiring, and I've cherished every moment of playing alongside them.

They've formed an unbreakable bond over the years, which has directly impacted how close I've gotten with Jeremy, Keenan, and Jordan—so much so that they all stood by my side on my wedding day. They have taught me invaluable life lessons, especially about grace in victory and defeat. I aspire to replicate their close-knit brotherhood in my own life, and I'm incredibly grateful for the warmth and wisdom family has brought into my life through football.

APPENDIX IV

THE FOLLOWING ARE the names of my teammates from our championship team in the fall of 2022 when we attended the Canadian Tournament of Champions. The African proverb is worth repeating; "If you want to go fast, go alone. If you want to go far go together." Thank you to the following men for allowing me to join them for the experience of a lifetime. Thank you for allowing me to be part of your "masterpiece."

Jeremy Kornelsen, Owen Kornelsen, Keenan Lehmann (the "Young Guns"): Every team needs the energy and talents of youth. These young men are wise beyond their years, and in their own way often carried the team with their big catches and timely big plays. It's beyond a privilege to watch these young guys grow to be mature, responsible young men. They inspire me.

Mike Nelson: Mike and I shared the quarterback duties. Mike made big throws every time we needed them, but more importantly, he's an incredible teammate. We made it work between us. Mike, you are a true champion. We wouldn't have raised the championship trophy without you.

Dave Robson: The captain of our defence. His solid football mind and leadership skills were evident from the first whistle on the first day. His efforts in the championship game were incredible. His leadership stood out, and he was not getting back on the plane to go home without the championship trophy. His will to win was paramount to our success.

Kevin Thompson ("KT") and Terence Gyselinck: I didn't know these guys very well before the tournament, but I had played against them. They both have one gear, and that is 100 per cent all the time. These are character guys, and they exemplified the traits of resiliency, perseverance, and character. Their toughness and team mentality were infectious. What a privilege to play with these guys.

Ev Jackson: A tremendous athlete who made the big plays when we needed them the most. These plays included his interception early in Game 1, which set the tone for the weekend, and his timely touchdown catches during the tournament. Another key piece in the makeup of our championship team.

Brandon Lebeau: He ran miles and miles over the three days chasing down quarterbacks. He was relentless, and his contributions were paramount to the success of our stellar defence. His energy and tenacity simply added to the mix of our championship defence.

Darryl Janzen: A young man who simply defines character with every step he takes on and off the field. His timely catches and consistent positive demeanour and steadiness were key to the team's success. It's no wonder why he has now been part of two national championship teams. Every team should have a Darryl in the huddle.

Jake Kornelsen, Henry Kornelsen, Sean Lehmann: These are three of the elder statesmen on the team. Their steady leadership qualities, competitive nature, and definition of a true teammate were instrumental in leading us to victory. I cannot describe my joy and how proud I am to have shared this incredible weekend with them.

I also want to make mention of our wives, who joined us on the trip and for their tremendous support. They were always there to cheer and encourage our team!

I have mentioned them before, but I want to name them again; Monica Kornelsen, Laura Kornelsen, Geni Lehmann, and my wife, Helen Bell.

These are special women who have followed us and supported us every step of the way. The are a key component of our team and always have been! Thank you, ladies, you are very special.

APPENDIX V

Things I Like, Things I Don't

THIS NEXT PART is for your leisure. I thought I would throw it in there in efforts of telling you more about me, according to me.

If you know me well, or perhaps you don't, I've made a list below of what I like and what I don't. Your list could be very different, and I respect that, no problem. Enjoy my list of likes and dislikes below. Have fun with it! I have nothing to hide.

Things I Like

- Time with my family and good friends.
- My church body.
- Sports—touch football is at the top of the list!
- A good meal—There is not much I don't like that is placed on my plate, and I have been blessed to be surrounded by some wonderfully talented cooks. Thank you, Helen, and my extended family.
- Dates with Helen.
- Gospel music, the hymns of old, and secular stuff from the '60s and '70s (Eagles, Neil Diamond, Bee Gees).
- People you can trust implicitly … and I know a few.
- Golfing with my buddies.
- Math. I am good with numbers! It's by far the sexiest subject on the planet.

- Deep conversations including constructive and respectful debate.
- Reading good books (my favourites are the Bible and books with leadership and Christian themes).
- Walking—sometimes alone and sometimes with Helen. I find it soothing and good for the soul. I think I do my best thinking and praying when I walk.
- Service opportunities.
- Laughing and making others laugh.
- Politics (I say this with some hesitation).
- Morning "strong" coffee, a must have with one-quarter cream and no sugar.
- Relaxing, golfing, and walking at the lake.
- Watching the news at night and searching for the truth between the lines.

Things I Do Not Like

- Gossip—I hate it, especially if I ever catch myself in it.
- Smoking—a costly bad habit in more ways than one!
- People who are always late; it's worse when I'm late! Let's be honest, to be late is not fashionable. It's rude and very disrespectful.
- Social media—It has some merit, but it certainly has its shortcomings. Definitely more shortcomings than merit. Think about it.
- Rap and heavy metal—It's not music. I would rather sit in a dental chair and have a root canal.
- Being "politically correct" (sometimes this is an oxymoron, if not always). What does it even mean?
- Condescending people—for which I have no patience or tolerance.
- People who are always right. Who are they kidding anyway? Nobody is undefeated!
- People who feel entitled.
- Cottage cheese—pass.
- Science fiction movies (*Star Wars* never did it for me).
- Impatient drivers.
- Watching the news at night (it's included in the other list as well).

Favourite Books

The Bible—several authors, and it is God-breathed. Please read this book, the # 1 bestseller of all time and for a reason. My favourite books in the Bible are Daniel and Proverbs.

A Game Plan for Life—So much good stuff in this book! I'll share a few favourite parts. John Wooden's father was one of his mentors in the book, the first one mentioned. His graduation gift from his father included a two-dollar bill and a card with a poem on one side and seven rules for living on the other:

1. Be true to yourself.
2. Make each day your masterpiece.
3. Help others.
4. Drink deeply from good books, including the Bible.
5. Make friendship a fine art.
6. Build a shelter against a rainy day.
7. Pray for guidance and give thanks for your blessings every day.

The above is wise and beautiful! What a gift to receive from your father.

Mission Drift

Start with Why

Live No Lies

The Ruthless Elimination of Hurry

I could make an extensive list but will limit myself to the above. I find reading is both relaxing and soothing, often good for the soul.

www.ingramcontent.com/pod-product-compliance
Lightning Source LLC
LaVergne TN
LVHW051553080426
835510LV00020B/2966